Arthur J Scanlan

The History of St. Joseph's Seminary of New York

Arthur J Scanlan

The History of St. Joseph's Seminary of New York

ISBN/EAN: 9783337426262

Printed in Europe, USA, Canada, Australia, Japan

Cover: Foto ©ninafisch / pixelio.de

More available books at **www.hansebooks.com**

THE HISTORY

— OF —

ST. JOSEPH'S SEMINARY

— OF —

NEW YORK

NEW YORK
THE CATHEDRAL LIBRARY ASSOCIATION
1896.

NOTE TO SECOND EDITION.

Many changes have occurred since the First Edition of this book was issued. The Right Rev. Monsignor Preston, D.D., (p. 3) and the Right Rev. Bishop of Curium (p. 10) have died. On page 11, 4th line, read "afterward Bishop to Clogher" for "present Bishop, etc.,". In our list of Priests ordained in St. Joseph's Seminary, Troy, it will be necessary to observe that the following are dead:

p. 32. REV. McCAULEY, JOHN,
p. 33. REV. BAXTER, HENRY
p. 33. REV. CALLAGHAN, MICHAEL,
p. 33. REV. GOODWIN, BERNARD,
p. 34. REV. BYRON JOSEPH,
p. 34. REV. FOY, WILLIAM,
p. 35. REV FITZHARRIS, JOHN,
p. 35. REV. HOGAN, WILLIAM,
p. 35. REV. FARRELL, WILLIAM,
p. 36. REV. KELLY, HUGH,
p. 36. REV ANTONI, CHARLES,
p. 37. REV. O'CALLAGHAN, GEORGE,
p. 37. REV. CLANCY, ANDREW,
p. 38. REV. McGILL, WILLIAM,
p. 39. REV. BUTLER WILLIAM,
p. 40. REV. KELLY WILLIAM.

The Very Rev. Monsignor Mooney (p. 71) has become a Right Rev. Domestic Prelate.

The thanks of the Catholics of New York are especially due to Mr. John Mullaly, whose self-sacrificing labors as editor of *The Seminary*, caused a knowledge of the work doing for the Seminary to be so widely known.

We are particularly indebted to Mr. Frank Parshley, Photographer, for his kindness in giving us permission to reproduce for this book his magnificent pictures of the new Seminary.

Preface.

The following history of the Diocesan Seminary of New York has been compiled from the most authentic records accessible. The compiler is much indebted to His Grace, the Most Rev. Archbishop of New York, to the Rt. Rev. Bishop of Rochester, the Rt. Rev. Monsignor Preston, D. D., the Rt. Rev. John M. Farley, D. D., Auxiliary Bishop of New York, the Rt. Rev. Charles E. McDonnell, D. D., Bishop of Brooklyn, for much of the information that is embodied herein. He has also consulted "The History of the Catholic Church in New York," by Archbishop Bayley, "The History of the Catholic Church in the United States," Vol. III., by Gilmary Shea, Scharf's "History of Westchester County," Bolton's "History of Westchester County," Hassard's "Life of Archbishop Hughes," together with the records of the Chancery Office of New York. To all these authorities he wishes to acknowledge his indebtedness. The book has had the advantage of thorough revision, and consequently is put forth as an accurate record of the history of the Seminary of this Diocese. For the photographs from which the engravings have been made, he is indebted to the Rev. John J. Scully, S. J., President of St. John's College, Fordham, the Rev. William Livingston, of the Troy Seminary, Mr. John D. Crimmins, Mr. William Schickel, and Mr. William Hurst.

ST. JOSEPH'S SEMINARY. FRONT VIEW.

PART I.

History of the Seminary of New York.

I.

History of the First Seminary.

In 1833, Bishop Dubois built at Nyack on the Hudson River, a college on the plan of Mount St. Mary's, Emmittsburg, combining both the theological and collegiate course of studies. The corner-stone of this, New York's first Seminary, was laid on the 29th of May, 1833, by the Bishop. The institution did not prosper, and when it was destroyed by fire before it was quite finished, the Bishop expressed himself, on the whole, as rather satisfied than discouraged. The future Cardinal, McCloskey, not yet ordained, was destined by Dr. Dubois to be the first President of the Nyack Seminary. In order to finish his studies he was allowed to go to Europe, with the understanding that he was to take charge of the Seminary on his return. A second attempt was made shortly afterwards to build a Diocesan Seminary in Brooklyn. The stone was transported from the ruins at Nyack to the site of the new Seminary. It would appear that Mr. Cornelius Heeney * had offered some lots for the erection of a college; but, as he afterwards was unwilling to give the proper deed until the building was completed, the project was abandoned. In the meantime, Bishop Hughes, then the coadjutor of Bishop Dubois, had set about founding a theological Seminary at Grovemount, Lafargeville, Jefferson County, in the extreme northwestern part of New York, near

* Mr. Cornelius Heeney was a distinguished Catholic, and benefactor of the Orphans. He lived in Water Street, New York, until 1835, when he made Brooklyn his home. His house was a home for orphans, and he always had some living with him, whose prosperity in life he secured as far as possible. Every year, he brought the children of the Orphan Asylums of New York to visit his orchard in Brooklyn when the fruit was ripe. When the Catholics in Brooklyn wished to build a church, he offered a site, and subsequently gave the ground for St. Paul's Church. In 1839, he gave the Orphan Asylum in Brooklyn $18,000. He was also one of the founders of the Catholic Half Orphan Asylum in New York. He died at the age of ninety-four, leaving his entire estate to the poor and the orphans.

the Thousand Islands, in the St. Lawrence River. Bishop Dubois approved the undertaking, because from his happy experience at Emmittsburg, he was in favor of placing Seminaries as far as possible from the excitements and temptations of large cities. Lafargeville was three hundred miles from New York, and well removed from all great lines of communication. The property consisted of four hundred and sixty acres of excellent lime-stone land, with buildings in quality superior, in extent not much inferior, to Mount St. Mary's. These buildings were put up in 1834 and 1835 by Mr. Lafarge, at a cost of $30,000. The land itself was valued at from $35 to $40 an acre; and the whole was purchased by Bishop Hughes for $20,000.

After the Brooklyn plan had been abandoned, it was determined to make the Lafargeville establishment a college for secular education as well as a theological school. It was opened under the name of "St. Vincent of Paul's Seminary," September 20th, 1838, by the Rev. Messrs. Guth,

Moran, and Heas, and three tutors. They began with six young men and two boys. A short trial convinced the Bishop that Lafargeville would never succeed as a house of general education. He sold this property to his brother, and it is still in the possession of the Hughes family. Shortly afterward he found a suitable place for the establishment of a new college at Fordham, in Westchester County, about ten miles from New York. The estate, called Rose Hill, was a beautiful spot. The buildings consisted of an unfinished stone house, on the summit of a gentle eminence, and an old wooden farm-house, which had been, in its day, rather a fashionable mansion. A beautiful lawn, some fifteen or twenty acres in extent, occupied the slope in front of these buildings, and along the edge of it was a fringe of magnificent elm trees, the seeds of which had been brought from Holyrood Palace. Behind the stone building lay a large and productive farm, and back of that a beautiful wood, through which ran the River Bronx. Rose Hill besides had many his-

ST. JOHN'S HALL, FORDHAM, N. Y. CITY.

torical associations, as it was near Fordham Heights, celebrated in Revolutionary History as part of the position occupied by General Washington before the Battle of White Plains in 1776; and a mound of earth, covering the remains of a number of soldiers, was a conspicuous spot on the north side of the lawn, seeming to indicate that a skirmish had taken place on or near the estate. While the American Congress was in session in New York just after the peace of 1783, Rose Hill was the residence of the celebrated Lady Mary Watts, the daughter of Lord Stirling, and the old farmhouse must have witnessed in those days many a brilliant scene of gaiety and fashion.

The cost of Rose Hill was about $30,000. To fit the buildings for the reception of students cost $10,000 more. The Bishop, who had not a penny to meet these expenses, concluded the bargain, and immediately opened subscriptions throughout the Diocese. A large part of the money was obtained in this way by voluntary subscription. The churches in the city of New York showed their confidence in him by subscribing at once more than ten thousand dollars. A considerable sum was collected in Europe, and the rest was finally raised by loans in small amounts, for which interest was paid at the rate of 5 per cent.

The Seminary was removed from Lafargeville to Fordham in the Autumn of 1840, and opened with fourteen Seminarists, Rev. Felix Vilanis being Superior; and the College was opened in June, 1841, with the following faculty:

President, and Professor of Rhetoric and Belles-lettres, REV. JOHN MCCLOSKEY, (afterwards Cardinal Archbishop of New York); *Vice-President, and Professor of Greek and Mathematics*, REV. AMBROSE MANAHAN, D. D.; *Professor of Moral Philosophy*, REV. FELIX VILANIS, D. D.; *Treasurer, and Professor of Natural Philosophy and Chemistry*, REV. EDWARD O'NEILL; *Professor of Spanish*, REV. BERNARD A. LLANEZ; *Professor of Latin*, MR. JOHN J. CONROY, (now Bishop of Curium); *Prefect of Discipline, and Professor of Book-keeping*, MR. JOHN HARLEY; *Professor of German*, MR.

REAR VIEW OF ST. JOHN'S HALL, FORDHAM, N. Y. CITY.

OERTEL; *Professor of French*, MR. MCDONALD.

There were, besides these, six tutors.

It had been Bishop Hughes' intention to make Father Donnelly, the present Bishop of Clogher, Ireland, the first president; but his Bishop refused to allow him to accept the position. Father McCloskey was, therefore, made president provisionally, he, in the meanwhile, remaining Pastor of St. Joseph's Church.

The Seminary was placed under the patronage of St. Joseph, the College under that of St. John the Baptist. The Seminarists occupied at first a small stone dwelling-house, west of the College. The large building afterwards used by the Seminary, and the church adjoining it, were begun in 1845. Bishop Hughes not only labored indefatigably to raise money for the foundation and support of St. Joseph's, but also devoted to that institution a considerable part of his own salary.

During the second year of its existence, the Seminary had thirty students, nineteen pursuing the theological course. St. John's College had fifty pupils, and soon gained the confidence of Catholic parents. One of its first presidents, the Rev. John Harley, a man of singular ability, and universally esteemed, did much to extend its influence.

As it was found impracticable to secure a permanent secular faculty, the Bishop determined to transfer the management to the Jesuit Fathers; and in the autumn of 1846, a number of them who had been previously employed in the diocese of Louisville, arrived and took charge of it. The State Legislature had granted a charter to the institution on the 17th of March, 1845, conferring university privileges upon it. The first commencement for conferring degrees, was held on the 15th of July, 1845, after which the College was committed to the Jesuits. The Rev. Auguste Thébaud was the first president under the Society. In 1851, he was succeeded by the Rev. John Larkin.

The following list of priests ordained at Lafargeville and Fordham from 1841 to 1853 taken from

SOUVENIR. 13

Bishop Bayley's History, will be of interest:

Rev. Miles Maxwell, Lafargeville and Fordham.
Rev. J. Mackay, Fordham.
Rev. B. L. Laniza, Lafargeville and Fordham.
Rev. Chas. D. McMullen, "
Rev. Carberry J. Byrne, Fordham.
Rev. Anthony Farley, Lafargeville and Fordham.

FORDHAM.

Rev. Francis Donahue.
Rev. Isaac P. Howel.
Rev. Michael McDonnell.
MOST REV. JAMES ROOSE-
   VELT BAYLEY.
Rev. William McClellan.
Rev. Michael Curran, Jr.
Rev. Michael Riordan.
Rev. John Hackett.
Rev. John Sheridan.
Rev. Thomas McElroy.
Rev. William O'Reilly.
Rev. Sylvester Malone.
Rev. Matthew Higgins.

Rev. George McCloskey.
Rev. Patrick Kenny.
RT. REV. F. P. McFAR-
   LAND.
Rev. Valentine Burgos.
Rev. Patrick McKenna.
Rev. John J. McMenomy.
RT. REV. WILLIAM QUINN.
Rev. Patrick Murphy.
Rev. James Hourigan.
Rev. Eugene Maguire.
Rev. Thomas Daly.
Rev. John Curoe.
Rev. Dennis Wheeler.

Rev. James O'Sullivan.
Rt. Rev. B. J. McQuaid.
Rev. John M. Murphy.
Rev. John Boyle.
Rev. Edward Reilly.
Rev. John Quinn.
Rev. Stephen Sheridan.
Rev. Thomas Dunn.
Rev. John Raufeisen.
Rev. Thomas Doran.
Rev. John Carroll.
Rev. Henry O'Neill.
Rev. Patrick McCarthy.
Rev. Michael Madden.
Rev. Hugh Sweeny.

Rev. John Comerford.
Rt. Rev. T. S. Preston.
Rev. John Regan.
Rev. Eugene Cassidy.
Rev. Thomas McLaughlin.
Rev. James Coyle.
Rev. Titus Joslin.
Rev. Cornelius Delahunty.
Rt. Rev. A. J. Donnelly.
Rev. Patrick Egan.
Rev. Bernard Farrell.
Rev. Patrick McGovern.
Rev. Thomas Mooney.
Rev. William Everett.
Rev. Francis McKeone.

The following list is from official records:

Rev. Brennan, James	Jan. 18, 1854.	
" Mahoney, Patrick	" " "	
" McCarron, Peter	" " "	
" O'Callaghan, Benjamin J.	" " "	
" Baldauf, Francis J.	Aug. 12, "	
" Campbell, John	" " "	

FORDHAM, (Continued).

Rev. Cannon, Cornelius	Aug. 12, 1854	
" Kelly, John A.	"	
" Lynch, Edward	"	
" McMahon, Philip	"	
" McNierney, Francis	" " "	
" Barry, John	Dec. 20,	
" McGean, Edward		
" Murray, John		
" Boyce, James	Aug. 15, 1855.	
" McEvoy, John	" " "	
" O'Donohue, Philip		
" McDermott, John		
" Magee, John	"	
" Brennan, Richard	Apr. 27, 1857	
" Byrne, Robert	" " "	
" Murphy, Peter		
" Slevin, Charles		
" Treanor, Thomas	"	
" Nelligan, William J.	June 9, "	
" Conron, James L.	May 3, 1858.	
" Doyle, John L.	" " "	

Rev. Clark, William (Hartford)   May 3, 1858
"   Hechinger, Anthony   "   "   "
"   Ferrall, Peter   June 28, 1859.
"   Orsenigo, John   "   "   "
"   Remsal, George A.   "   "
"   Woods, Joseph P.   "   "
"   Lenihan, Francis J.   "
"   Sheridan, Philip   "
"   O'Hara, Oliver   "
"   Farrell, Christopher A.   Oct. 15, 1860.
"   O'Callaghan, Cornelius Jas. "   "   "

The Rt. Rev. Bernard J. McQuaid, D. D., Bishop of Rochester, furnishes the following interesting information concerning the Diocesan Seminary of New York, that existed at the present site of the Cathedral :

"The students were removed from Fordham to the old building on 5th Avenue and 50th Street, in January, 1844. The Rev. Fathers Penco and Borgna, Lazarists, were Superiors and Professors. The students numbered about twenty, few of whom are now living. Mr. Bayley, after-

PARTERRE, REAR OF ST. JOHN'S HALL, FORDHAM, N. Y. CITY.

wards Archbishop of Baltimore, here made his immediate preparation for ordination. The Seminarists returned to Fordham for the next term in September. Thus the Seminary was kept up at 50th Street for nearly six months. The students were directed, when they went out for a walk on Thursday afternoons and Sundays, not to go to the city, and, that no mistake might be made, they were told not to go nearer than 27th Street. Of all the Seminarists that were there, the Rev. James Hourigan of Binghamton N. Y.; the Rev. John Sheridan of Cleveland, O., and the Rev. Sylvester Malone, of Brooklyn, and myself are the only ones living."

The Seminary continued at Fordham, under the charge of the Jesuit Fathers, until 1862, when it was closed in consequence of the disturbed condition of affairs that followed the breaking out of the war of the Rebellion, whose true magnitude had just then dawned on the people of the North. In the same year Archbishop Hughes, on the recommendation of the Rev.

Peter Havermans, purchased the property, now known as St. Joseph's Provincial Seminary, at Troy, N. Y. The history of this property is related by the Archbishop in a letter:

"About the year 1850, the Methodists determined to rival the other denominations by founding a great University in the city of Troy, New York State. It is said that their subscription list amounted to half a million of dollars. At all events, they purchased a piece of ground, on a beautiful site called Mount Ida, consisting of thirty-seven acres of land situated almost in the centre of Troy, and erected upon it an imposing educational building of 360 feet front, four stories high, and 60 feet deep, with architectural adornments of turrets, etc. The building, independent of the ground, cost $197,000. It contained altogether about three hundred rooms for students.* There are departments for philoso-

---

* To those who know the Seminary of Troy these figures are misleading. Bishop Hughes, of course, wrote from hearsay, as he had not yet inspected the building. At present there are only ninety-one rooms reserved for students, and these will accommodate only one

phical experiments, a museum, library, and a chapel for the accommodation of six hundred attendants,* together with a very good organ. I purchased the whole property last week, including furniture, the organ, etc., for $60,000."

Local traditions relate many humorous stories of the sale, and of the conversion of a Methodist into a Roman Catholic seminary.

This institution although not in the Diocese of New York, was at that time the central point of Archbishop Hughes' Ecclesiastical Province,† there being a railroad to it from the home of each of his suffragans, as well as from his own. In purchasing it, his intention was to place it under the management of the Sulpitians of Paris, or some other association devoted to the education of priests that would take charge of it, and to main-

hundred and fifty-eight or sixty at most. There were many changes required to make the building suitable for a Seminary.

* The chapel, as arranged at present, can accommodate only about three hundred.

† The Metropolitan See of New York included at that time the present Province of Boston.

tain it as the Ecclesiastical Seminary of the Province of New York. There was considerable difficulty about the preliminaries for the establishment of this Seminary. At one time the Archbishop was on the point of selling the property and founding a new institution at Fordham, about half a mile from St. Joseph's. He went so far as to request a gentleman to negotiate in his own name for the purchase of a certain piece of land which seemed to be especially well suited to his purpose, but before long the difficulties connected with the Troy scheme were overcome. This was Archbishop Hughes' last work.

The management of the new Seminary was offered to the Sulpitians, but the Superior of that congregation felt constrained to decline the offer, fearing that there was not room enough for a new Seminary between Baltimore and Montreal. The fact that the Sulpitians now have charge of Brighton, and are to take charge of the new St. Joseph's, attest the wonderful growth of the Church in this district. By the zealous labors of

STATUE OF ST. JOSEPH, FRONT OF SEMINARY.

the late Cardinal McCloskey, then Bishop of Albany, through the kindness of Mgr. Delebecque, Bishop of Ghent, Belgium, professors from the University of Louvain were found who were willing to undertake the delicate task. The self-sacrifice and zeal manifested by these gentlemen, the first professors of St. Joseph's, cannot be too highly praised. Coming utter strangers into a foreign land, entirely unacquainted with the language and customs, their task was certainly a difficult one.

Owing to important changes that had to be made in the building to adapt it for use as a Catholic seminary, it was scarcely ready for occupation when they arrived. It was opened, as the Seminary of St. Joseph, in the month of October, 1864, with a faculty consisting of a rector, and three professors from Louvain, and two from the clergy of Boston and New York. The students numbered sixty, and represented the various dioceses in the ecclesiastical province of New York.

Archbishop Hughes died on Sunday, January 3d, 1864, before the work he had undertaken was successfully put in operation. On the 1st of December, 1864, his successor, Archbishop McCloskey, in the presence of the suffragan Bishops of Boston, Hartford, Burlington, and Portland, and the administrator of Albany, solemnly dedicated the new Seminary, placing it under the protection of St. Joseph.

Three years later, the number of students was one hundred and forty, and ever since it has varied from one hundred to one hundred and sixty. The needs of dioceses, changing with various circumstances of immigration and ecclesiastical partition, have caused a corresponding change in the number of representatives from dioceses. The opening of the Seminary at Brighton drew off all the students from the Province of Boston. The spiritual wants of the French Canadians caused the Bishops of many of the dioceses of New England to send their subjects to Montreal. New York has always had, and, of course, has now, the preponderating number of students. From its opening until January, 1891, St. Joseph's Seminary has matriculated 1036 students, of whom 625, after the regular course, have been ordained priests in the Seminary chapel, or at home, 140 are now at the Seminary, the others having either died, or been ordained elsewhere, or abandoned their studies. There are, at the present writing, (June, 1891), about 200 students of St. Joseph's laboring in the diocese of New York; 60 in Albany; 69 in Boston; 48 in Rochester; 13 in Hartford; 12 in Springfield; 14 in Ogdensburg; 3 in Portland; 8 in Peoria; 4 in Burlington; 30 in Syracuse; 5 in Providence; 5 in Manchester; 3 in Trenton; 1 in Detroit; 2 in Denver; 1 in Buffalo; 1 in Louisville; 1 in Chicago; 2 with the Jesuits; 1 with the Redemptorists *

There have not been many changes in the original faculty, as will be seen from the following :

The different Faculties of St. Joseph's Seminary, Troy, N. Y.

1864. VERY REV. CANON LOUIS VANDENHENDE

* These statistics were prepared with much labor by the Very Rev. H. Gabriels, S. T. D., President of St. Joseph's Provincial Seminary, Troy, N. Y.

D. D. President, Director and Professor of Canon Law, Church History and Sacred Eloquence.

REV. CHARLES ROELANTS, S. T. B., Prof. Sacred Scripture.

REV. PETER A. PUISSANT, S. T. B. Prof. Philosophy.

REV. ALEXANDER SHERWOOD HEALY, Prof of Moral Theology.

REV. PATRICK WILLIAM TANDY, Procurator

REV. HENRY GABRIELS S. T. L. Prof Dogmatic Theology.

1865. REV. MICHAEL MULLEN, Prof. of Philosophy (in place of Fr. Puissant, who took Moral)

REV. PETER A PUISSANT, Prof. Moral, in place of Fr. HEALY, who became Director.

1866. REV. JOHN EDWARDS, Procurator (place of Fr. TANDY)

1867. REV. THOMAS KENNY, Prof. of Philosophy in place of Fr. MULLEN—resigned.

1868. REV. PETER. A. SCHMIDT, Prof. of Church History.

Rev. Hugh Shields, S. T. B. Prof. Philos. place of Fr. Kenny resigned.

1869. Rev. John McLoughlin, Director—place of Fr. Healy, resigned.

1870. Rev. Henry Gabriels, S. T. L. Took Church History in place of Fr. Schmidt, resigned.

1871. Rev. Henry Gabriels, S. T. D. President, (place of Fr. Vandenhende)

Rev. Augustine Fivez, S. T. L. Dogma. (place of Fr. Gabriels)

Rev. James S. M. Lynch. Director—place of Fr. McLoughlin, resigned.

Rev. Joseph F. Mooney. Prof. of Philos. (place of Fr. Shields, resigned.)

1872. Rev. Philip Garrigan. Prof. of Sacred Eloquence. Director, place of Fr. Lynch resigned.

1873. Rev. Peter A. Puissant Procurator, place of Fr. Edwards, resigned.

1875. James S. M. Lynch. Director for second

time—place of FR. GARRIGAN, recalled by his Bishop, for diocesan duties.

REV. EDWARD A. DUNPHY, Prof. Sacred Eloquence, and minor Branches.

1879. REV. CORNELIUS MAHONY, D. D. Prof. of Philos., place of FR. MOONEY and Sacred Eloquence, place of FR. DUNPHY.

1880. REV. JOHN F. WOODS, D. D. Director in place of FR. LYNCH and Prof. Sacred Eloquence.

1883. REV. REMY LAFORT, S. T. L. Prof. of Canon Law and Introduction to Sacred Scripture.

1884. REV. DANIEL BURKE, D. D. Prof. of Philosophy place of DR. MAHONY and Prof. of Sacred Eloquence.

REV. WM. A. MCDONALD. Director, place of DR. WOODS.

1886. (February) REV. MICHAEL J. CONSIDINE, director place of FR MCDONALD; Prof. of Natural Sciences, and Sacred Eloquence.

1887. REV. WILLIAM H. MURPHY, Professor of

Logic and Metaphysics, place of DR.
BURKE.

1889. REV. WILLIAM LIVINGSTON. Director, place of FR. CONSIDINE. Prof. of Natural Sciences, and Sacred Eloquence.

1890.—1891. REV. JAMES FITZSIMMONS, S. T. B. Prof. of Logic, place of REV. FR. MURPHY, who took Metaphysics, place of Fr. Lafort, who took Scripture, place of Fr. Roelants resigned.

1892. REV. JOSEPH F. DELANY, D. D., succeeded FR. FITZSIMMONS as Professor of Logic, the latter taking Metaphysics.

In 1871, Canon Vandenhende, who was very much beloved by the students, and highly esteemed by all who knew him, returned to Belgium, and was made Canon and Magnus Pœnitentiarius of the Cathedral of Ghent. About the same time, the course of studies was lengthened, and a new branch introduced, viz: Sacred Eloquence.

Father Roelants, Professor of Sacred Scripture, and dear to all who listened to his clear, interesting, and, frequently, eloquent comments upon the sacred text, much to the regret of the former and of the present students, resigned his professorship in the summer of 1890, and was made Canon of the Cathedral of Ghent. With these exceptions, the members of the original faculty are still at St. Joseph's.

And now, before passing to the New Seminary, let us in the following chapter, give a parting glance at the old.

BOARD WALK, REAR OF ST. JOSEPH'S SEMINARY, TROY, N. Y.

II.

The Seminary at Troy.

St. Joseph's Provincial Seminary at Troy, N. Y., stands on the most beautiful part of Ida Hill, overlooking the compactly built city that presides over the head-waters of navigation of the Hudson River. The sounds of life from the bustling city reach the crest of the high hill with softened murmur, and at that elevation, the roar of busy trade, the sharply tolling bell of a passing train, the shriek of a locomotive on the farther hills, dashing along, groaning with the weight of its heavy cars, become romantic. At certain seasons of the year, from April till July, and from September till November, the Seminary grounds were really beautiful, and will be held in pleasant memory by those who have been students at St. Joseph's.

The pale mists that rose steaming from the Mohawk Valley, as they floated lazily upwards were tinted with the splendors of the rising sun. At eventide, the western heavens deepened with ever varying colors. The placid Mohawk lay like a silver ribbon between its rich green banks, taking on the shifting hues of evening and morning. Northward could be seen the mills and churches, and spires of busy Cohoes, picturesque at that distance; while to the south rose the Cattskills' massive blue wall, its broken line now wreathed in purple mists, now tricked out in the golden splendor of gorgeous day. In the cool eventide of the long spring days, the odors of fruit blossoms and lilacs mingled with the indescribable sweetness of grass and shrub and new turned earth. The interlocking branches of fruit trees, white with the clustering blossoms, roofed over the well kept paths, which traversed the spacious grounds rendered beautiful by the patient labors of the humble brothers. On all sides lay the green sward bristling with spears of timothy,

SHRINE OF SACRED HEART, ON THE GROUNDS.

shaded by clumps of red top, and softened by the snow of fallen blossoms. Through a lovely vale trickled a tiny brook overhung with weeping willows, whose tender leaves filled the branches with green-gold stars. Nestling amid a thick shrubbery is the shrine of the Sacred Heart, erected by the Trojan students as a token of their love for the Sacred Heart of their Master. In the center of a pretty parterre, on the plateau immediately in front of the Seminary chapel, stands a statue of St. Joseph, placed there by the class of 1870, on the occasion of the tenth anniversary of their ordination, in acknowledgment of how much they owed to the patronage of this great saint.

III.

Priests Ordained in Troy for the Diocese of New York

In order to complete our history of the Seminary, we append a list of those students ordained after their course in St. Joseph's Seminary, Troy, N. Y., for the archdiocese of New York.

Rev. Hussey, William J.	Dec. 17, 1864.[1]	Died 1865.		
" Fitzsimmons, James,	July,	1865.		
" O'Hare, Hugh,	"	"		
" Edwards, John,	Aug. 21, 1866.			
" Brogan, John,	Nov. 20, 1866.			
" McCauley, John,	"	"	"	
" McEvoy, Michael,	"	"	"	" 1884.
" Flannelly, William,	Jun. 15, 1867.		" 1884.	
" Lings, Albert,	"	"	"	
" Neade, Thomas,	"	"	"	" 1873.
" Brennan, Michael,	Dec. 21, 1867.			
" Daly, Patrick,	"	"	"	" 1877.
" Dougherty, James,	"	"	"	
" Earley, Terence,	"	"	"	
" Quinn, John,	"	"	"	" 1876.
" Murphy, George,	Jun. 6, 1868.		" 1882.	
" Galligan James,	"	"	"	
" Keenan, James,	"	"	"	" 1874.
" Loughran, Patrick,	"	"	"	" 1876.

[1] Had entered as deacon Oct. 1864.

Rev. McCourt, Peter,	Jun. 6, 1868.	Died 1877
" O'Farrell, Michael,	" " "	
" Ducey, Thomas,	Dec. 19, 1868.	
" Dunphy, Edward,	" " "	" 1885.
" Galligan, Bartholom.	Dec. 19, 1868.	" 1883.
" Martin, Francis,	" " "	" 1874.
" Brophy, Martin,	May, 22, 1869.	" 1890.
" Baxter, Henry,	" " "	
" Callaghan, Michael,	"	
" Henry, John,		
" McClancy, John,		
" McNamee, John,		
" Welsh, Thomas,		" 1871.
Brady, William,	Nov. 16,	
Mullen, James,	" " "	
" Canary, Andrew,	Jun. 11, 1870.	
" Hayne, Joseph,	" " "	
Healy, Patrick,	" "	1889.
Mee, James,	"	
Meister, Isidor,	" "	
O'Flaherty, Martin,	"	1881
" Phelan, Michael,	"	
" Kean, John,	" 3, 1871.	
" Clancy, James,	" "	1872.
" Corley, Charles,	"	
" Goodwin, Bernard,	"	
" Mooney, Joseph,		
" O'Neil, William,	" "	
Very Rev. Penny, William,	"	

Rev.	Rigney, Patrick,	Jun. 3, 1871.	Died 1885.
"	Lynch, Thomas,	July. "	
"	Byron, Joseph,	Dec. 23, 1871.	
"	Hughes, Nicholas,	" " "	
"	Brophy, Patrick,	May 25, 1872,	" 1874.
"	Flood, James,	" " "	
"	Keogan, John,	" " "	
"	Lynch, John,	" " "	
"	McQuirk, John,	" " "	
"	Malone, Patrick,	" " "	" 1886
"	O'Kelly, William,	" "	
"	Gordon, Henry,	" " "	
"	Campbell, Joseph,	Dec. 21, "	
"	Corkery, Daniel,	" " "	" 1891.
"	Donovan, Cornelius,	" " "	" 1887.
"	Molloy, Anthony,	" " "	
"	Power, James,	" " "	
"	Westerman, James,	" " "	
"	McGinley, Edward,	June 7, 1873.	
"	Newman, Michael,	" " "	" 1887.
"	O'Gorman, Edward,	" "	
"	Salter, John,	" "	
"	Smyth, Eugene,	" "	
"	Colton, John,	Dec. 20, "	" 1878.
"	Foy, William,	" "	
"	McGivney, John,	" "	" 1881.
"	Riordan, John,	Mar. 19, 1874.	" 1887.
"	Corr, John,	May 30, "	1875.
"	Cronin, Daniel,	" " "	

SOUVENIR. 35

Rev. Farrell, Peter,	May, 30, 1874			
" Fitzharris, John,	" " "			
" Morris, John.	" "	Died 1886.		
" Ward, William	" "			
" Hogan, William,	Dec. 19, "			
" Doyle, John,	May 22, 1875.	1878.		
" Egan, Joseph	" " "			
" Hayes, James,	" "			
" Hurley, John,	" " "	" 1891.		
" Kiely, James,	" "			
" McCabe, Hugh,	" "			
" Martin, Patrick,	" " "			
" Farrell, William,	Dec 18, "			
" McSwiggan, Michael,	" " "	" 1890.		
" Montgomery, Michael,	" " "			
Colton, Charles,	Jun. 10, 1876.			
Nagle, Stephen,	" " "	" 1881.		
Dougherty, Maurice,	" "	" 1890.		
Crosby, James,	"			
" O'Hanlon, Thomas,	" " "	" 1883.		
" McCloskey, Patrick,	" "	" 1877.		
" Grady, John,	" "	" 1888.		
" Meister, Filibert,	" " "			
" Lane, Michael,	Dec. 23, "	" 1888.		
" Slattery, Edward,	" " "			
" Ahern, Philip,	May. 26, 1877.			
" Fitzpatrick, Tobias,	" " "	" 1880.		
" Mayer, John,	" "			
" O'Hare, John,	" " "			

Rev.	Quinn, Michael,	May 26, 1876.	Die	1882.
"	Boddy, William,	Dec. 22, "	"	1890.
"	Byrnes, Edward,	" " "		
"	Connick, Patrick,	Dec. 22, 1877		
	Hoey, Joseph,	" " "		
"	Kuhnen, Matthew,	" " "		
"	McCormick, Daniel,	" " "		
"	McGare, Thomas,	" " "		
"	Ward, Daniel,	" " "		
"	Bigley, Joseph,	" 21, 1878.		
"	Byrnes, James P.	" " "		
"	Dunphy, Thomas,	" " "		
"	Dunphy, William,	" " "	"	1891
"	Henry, Michael,	" "		
"	McCorry, Patrick,	" " "		
	Dixon, Felix,	" " "	"	1883.
"	Cunnion, Malachy,	Jan. 26, 1879.		
"	Kelly, Hugh,	" " "		
"	Donlin, George,	Mar. 29, "		
	Parks, Charles,	" " "		
"	Sweeney, Edwin,			
"	Duffy, Bernard,	Jun. 7, "		
	McNamee, Peter,	" "		
"	Smyth, Thomas,	" " "		
"	Antoni, Charles,	Dec. 20, "		
"	Brennan, Joseph,	" " "		
"	Brophy, John,	" " "		1891.
"	Byrnes, James M.	" "		
	Costello, Luke,	"	"	1883.

Rev. McCabe, Patrick,   Dec. 20, 1879.   Died 1890.
  " Haran, Michael,   "   "   "
  " Kellner, John,   "   "
Rev. Wolff, John,   Dec. 20, 1879.   " 1887.
  " Leahy, David.   May 22, 1880.
  " McCarthy, James,   "   "   "
  " Creeden, John.   Dec. 18, "
  " McLaughlin, James,   "   "   "
  " McCluskey, Thomas,   "   "   "
  " Cummiskey, James,   "   "   "   " 1885.
  " Meredith, Charles.   June 11, 1881.
  " O'Callaghan, George,   "   "   "
  " Magann, Peter.   "   "   "   " 1888.
  " Quinn, Thomas.   "   "   "
  " Rigney, James,   "   "   "
  " Clancy, Andrew.   Dec. 17. "
  " Donahue, James.   "   "   "
  " Kelly, James.   "   "
  " Flannelly, Joseph,   "   "   "
  " McEvoy, Michael,   "   "   "
  " Gallagher, John,   "   "   "
  " Waters, Arthur.   "   "
  " Kenny Michael,   "   "   "
  " O'Meara, Patrick.   "   "   "
  " Considine, Michael,   June 3. 1882.
  " Feely, Joseph,   "   "   "
  " Carr, John,   Dec. 23. "
  " Murphy, William,   "   "   "
  " Xavier, Henry,   "   "   "

Rev. Burns, Richard,	May 19, 1883.	
" McGill, William,	" " "	
" Evers, Luke,	" "	
" Boyle, John,	Dec. 22, "	
" Parker, Moses,	" " "	
" Weir, John,	" " "	
" McKenna, John,	June 7, 1884.	
" Owens, John,	" " "	
" Mulhern, Michael,	" " "	
" Shine, Eugene,	" " "	
" Aylward, Michael,	Dec. 20, "	
" Clancy, Patrick,	" "	
" Fitzsimons, Patrick,	" "	
" Kelly Francis,	" " "	
" Lonargan, John,	" " "	
" Moore, Francis,	" "	
Power, John,	" "	
Wallace, Thomas,	" " "	
Welsh, Michael,	" " "	
Cusack, Thomas,	May, 30, 1885.	
" Galligan, Thomas,	" " "	
" O'Connell, Morgan,	"	
Coyle, Dennis,	Dec. 19.	
Daly, William,	· "	
Jones, Francis,	" "	
" Lénès, Francis,	" "	
" Mechler, Joseph,		
" Quinn, John,	" "	
" Irving, Thomas,	June 19, 1886. Died 1887.	

SOUVENIR. 39

Rev. McMahon, Joseph,	June 19, 1886.	
" Murphy, Edward,	" " "	
" Jackson, William,	" " "	
" Reinhart, Nicholas,	" " "	
" Brady, Bernard,	Dec. 18, "	
" Cullum, Hugh,	" " "	
" Donnelly, James,	" " "	
" Kinkead, Thomas,	" " "	
" Sheahan, Joseph,	" "	
" Somers, Edward,	" " "	
Higgins, Edward,	June 4, 1887.	
" Schwinn, John,	" " "	
Beaudet, Cyriacus,	Dec. 17,	
" Briody, John,	" " "	
" Chidwick, John,	" "	
" Dougherty, William,	" " "	
" Fagan, Francis,	" " "	
Fenton, James,	" " "	
Livingston, William,	"	
Morris, John,	" "	
Murray, Lawrence,	" "	
O'Keefe, Thomas,	" "	
" Hulse, Francis,	" "	Died 1890
" Pellieux, Augustine,	June 24, 1888,	
" O'Shaughnessy, John,	" " " "	1890.
" Braun, John,	Dec. 22,	
Butler, William,	" "	
Fremel, Francis,		
" Guinevan, Peter,		

Rev. McCue, Edward,	Dec.	22,	1888.
" Myhan, Thomas,	"	"	"
" O'Dwyer, Daniel,	"	"	"
" Roach, John,	"	"	
Feehan Daniel,	June	24,	1889
" Reilly, Bernard,	"	"	"
" Fitzsimmons, James,	Oct.	28,	"
" Kelly, William,	"	"	"
" Dooley, James	Dec.	21,	"
" Duffy, Michael,	"	"	"
" Holden, Edward,	"	"	"
" McCabe, James,	"		"
" Meade, John,	"		"
" Murphy, Thomas,	"		
" Ronayne, Patrick,	"	"	"
" Minogue, Patrick,	"	"	"
' Brady, Bernard,	Dec.	20,	1890.
" Spellman, Peter,	"	"	"
" Conway, John,	May	23,	1891.
" Cunniff, Michael,	"	"	"
" Donlin, Thomas,	"	"	"
" Goggin, James,	"		
" Hayes, William,	"	"	
Heafy, Thomas.	"		
" Keenan, Thomas,	"	"	"
" Lennon, John,	"	"	
" Mangan, James,	"		"
" O'Connor, Thomas,	"		"
" Ryan, John,	"	"	"
" Shine, Michael	"		

Rev.	Mallon, John J.,	Dec.	19,	1891.
"	Strezelecki, John H.,	"	"	"
"	Drain, Patrick H.,	Jan.	24,	1892.
"	Breslin, Patrick A.,	June	15,	"
"	Dooley, John A.,	"	"	
"	Galligan, Bartholomew F.,			"
"	Keliher, Michael F.,			
"	Kelahan, John F.,			
"	McDonald, Joseph V.,	"		
"	McKenna, Charles B.,*	"		
"	Murphy, Charles T.,	"	"	
"	Quinn, William,			
"	Thornton, Thomas A.,	"	"	
"	Hayes, Patrick J.,	Sept.	8,	"
"	Smith, Joseph F.,	"	"	"
"	Fitzpatrick, Malick J.,	Dec.	17.	"
"	Flood, Thomas F.,	"	"	"
"	Horan, Michael F.,	"	"	"
"	Kenny, Arthur J.,	"	"	"
"	McGuire, John F.,	"	"	"
"	Malloy, James F.,	"	"	"
"	Meehan, William F.,	"	"	"
"	O'Connell, Daniel A.,	"	"	"
"	Reilly, Thomas J.,	"	"	"
"	Brown, James J.,	June	24,	1893.
"	Dowling, John F.,	"	"	"
"	Gallagher, Michael P.,	"	"	"
"	Murray, David A.,	"	"	"

* Died June 15, 1893.

Rev.	Aylward, James N.,	May	19,	1894.
"	Crowley, Cornelius F.,	"	"	"
"	Crowley, Cornelius J.,	"	"	"
"	Cusack, Andrew F.,	"	"	"
"	Doyle, Thomas J.,	"	"	"
"	Driscoll, Timothy M.,	"	"	"
"	Fay, John J.,	"	"	"
"	Gibbons, Daniel A.	"	"	"
"	McNamara, James F.,	"	"	"
"	Nowak, Stanislaus J.,	"	"	"
"	Sullivan, Francis J.,	"	"	"
"	Keane, James J.,	Dec.	23,	"
"	Bergan, Joseph E.,	"	22,	"
"	O'Hanlon, Philip,	"	"	"
"	Strack, Otto,	"	"	
"	Pauli, Charles,	"	"	"
"	Walsh, Michael,	"	"	"
"	Carey, Patrick E.,	June	8,	1895.
"	Collins, James A.,	"	"	"
"	Donahue, Joseph P.,	"	"	"
"	Harrington, John J.,	"	"	"
"	Hickey, John J.,	"	"	"
"	Kelly, Thomas B.,	"	"	"
"	McKenna, Bernard F.,	"	"	"
"	Meehan, John F.,	"	"	"
"	St. John, William T.,	"	"	"
"	Weir, Robert A.,	"	"	"
"	Cusack, Louis M.,	Dec.	21,	1895.

THE FINAL FUNCTION AT ST. JOSEPH'S, TROY, N. Y.

Rev.	Cusack, Peter P.,	Dec.	21,	1895.
"	Mulcahy, William J.,	"	"	"
"	Brehney, James H.,	May	30,	1896.
"	Cushman, Joseph G.,	"	"	"
"	Dunn, John J.,	"	"	"
"	Gilmartin, Terence E.,	"	"	"
"	Gleeson, Matthew C.,	"	"	"
"	Halloran, Edward F.,	"	"	"
"	Kenny, Arthur J.,	"	"	"
"	Leonard, Edward F.,	"	"	"
"	Lyman, Thomas F.,	"	"	"
"	Maher, John J.,	"	"	"
"	O'Connor, David F.,	"	"	
"	O'Sullivan, Edward F.,	"	"	"
"	Owens, Thomas F.,	"	"	"
"	Phelan, Thomas P.,	"	"	"
"	Power, James J.,	"	"	"
"	Quinn, Daniel A.,	"	"	
"	Talbot, James A.,	"	"	"
"	Wilson, John J.,	"	"	"

IV.

History of the New Seminary Grounds.

The work for the welfare of the diocese that Archbishop Hughes began in founding the great Cathedral which shall be his everlasting monument, Archbishop Corrigan hopes to complete by building a diocesan Seminary which shall be worthy of the diocese whose destinies have been committed to his guidance. Keenly appreciating the fact that the care of the formation and the education of the clergy is of all the cares of the bishop the greatest and the most important ; endeavoring to adapt the discipline and the rules imposed upon clerics in the seminary to those of the Council of Trent ; wishing to give his seminarists the means for cultivating piety and abundant virtue, and desirous of encouraging the study of the highest sciences it has always been his hope to build within the limits of his diocese a Seminary of which the Catholics of New York could be justly proud. The inconvenience of the location of the Seminary at Troy, the rigorous climate, of the place, and moreover the necessity of having the institution under his immediate supervision were the motives that determined him to take immediate action. In doing this he was especially moved by a petition presented by his clergy in the Fifth Diocesan Synod, representing the many disadvantages of having to go to Troy for their Retreats. The Archbishop much to the joy of the priests, announced on that occasion that he hoped soon to build a Seminary within the limits of our own diocese. A competent Committee of priests, aided by the valuable assistance and advice of experienced laymen was appointed to secure a site. After examining many localities, they bought a farm at Scarborough, on the Hudson. The place however was found unsatisfactory on account of the inadequate means of access and the undesirable surroundings. The Committee resumed their labors and after examining all the available sites within the neighborhood of New York, they finally, through the agency of Mr. Georges Lespinasse purchased Valentine Hill, a plot of ground in the second ward of the city of Yonkers, lying between Valentine Street, Jerome Ave., Mile Square road, the land of James Gordon Bennett, and Midland Ave.

Valentine Hill is a high ridge bordering Mile Square on the west.* Its summit affords one of the finest views in Westchester County. On all sides is a fertile country, the gentle slopes of the hillsides covered with beautiful trees. Woodlands abound; while along the lovely, romantic country roads that meet here and stretch

---

* On the east side of the town of Yonkers bounded by the Bronx River is situated an attractive piece of land called Mile Square, lying principally in a beautiful valley watered by the river and sheltered by picturesque hills. This tract was exempted out of the great Manorial Patent of 1693, and appears originally to have formed a part of the possession of the Doughtys of Flushing; as we find John Doughty of that place, in 1685, selling four acres of land here in *one square mile* to Francis French and Ebenezer Jones and John Wascott.

away on all sides, stately residences and comfortable farm houses dot the landscape. Eastward lies an extensive country of hills, woods and valleys reaching with a gentle succession of undulations the Long Island Sound, whose waters, sparkling in the sunlight and white with the frequent sail, carry the eye to a chain of light blue hills bounding the distant horizon. To the southeast extends the flourishing village of Mount Vernon, its church spires standing out prominently. Northward are the Tuckahoe Hills as far as the eye can see, while westward the Yonkers ridge, crowned with lofty trees whose openings reveal here and there a glimpse of the Hudson valley, leads up to the dark wall of the Palisades, stretching in majestic grandeur away to the North. Below the Hill is a valley of rich rolling land watered by Tippet's brook and beautifully wooded. The old Croton Aqueduct winds along the foot of the Hill while further west can be seen the New Aqueduct.

The land known as the Valentine Farm, and, particularly, this Valentine's Hill with which we are concerned, belonged under the Crown to the estate of Frederick Philipse, Esq., and formed part of the manor of Philipsburg.* When Frederick Philipse was attainted, his estate was sequestrated. On May 18, 1786, Isaac Stoutenburgh and Philip Van Cortlandt, commissioners of forfeiture, conveyed 238 acres to Thomas Valentine, for the consideration of £2380. Thomas Valentine in his will, dated July 15, 1800, gave the farm on which he lived himself, *i. e.* Valentine's Hill, to his son Nathaniel, who in turn bequeathed it by will, dated May 29, 1837 to his son Elijah Valentine. A portion of it was conveyed on June 25, 1860 to John R. Haywood, a connection of the Valentines by marriage, it would appear: he conveying it to Mary A. Valentine and receiving in return a mortgage of $15,840. Haywood afterwards sued Mary

---

* The Philipse Manor House is the present City Hall of Yonkers. A tablet erected therein says that it was erected in 1682; that the Manor of Philipsburg was erected in 1693; confiscated by act of the Legislature of New York in 1779, and sold in 1785. It was used as a private residence until 1868, when it became the property of the city of Yonkers.

A. Valentine, and in pursuance of a judgment of the Supreme Court, bought back the property which he afterwards sold on May 4, 1863, to Susan Valentine. Her son, Nathaniel, and her daughter, Harriett A. Burtis, became possessed of equal shares in it by the demise of Susan Valentine. In October 30, 1882, Harriett sold her interest to Nathaniel who thus became possessed of the entire property. Valentine Hill, therefore, with the adjoining land, has been occupied by the Valentine family for nearly one hundred and ten years. There was an old burying ground in the immediate neighborhood where are interred the remains of Colonel Thomas Farringdon, of New-York City, and several members of the Valentine and Brown families. This burying ground is now included in the Woodlawn Cemetery.

The Valentines wishing to dispose of a portion of their land which had become very valuable by reason of its proximity to the city, conveyed, on March 6, 1890, the several parcels of land containing respectively, 6.251 acres, 14.047 acres, and

32.911 acres to MICHAEL A. CORRIGAN, for the sum of sixty-four thousand, one hundred and forty-six dollars, and seventy-seven cents. ($64,146.77).

Valentine's Hill, like the grounds of the old Seminary at Fordham, has many historical associations.

When the British army, in October 1776, occupied Westchester County, from New Rochelle to White Plains, the American armies moved rapidly by forced marches from Harlem Heights along the Tuckahoe Road, their march occupying from October 12th, to October 21st. The Brigade commanded by Brigadier General Lord Stirling was pushed first to the Mile Square, and afterwards to the White Plains. Two regiments of the Massachusetts militia, under Major-General Lincoln, were sent up the Hudson river to watch the movements of the British ships, and prevent the landing of men, while the headquarters of that division, and probably its two remaining regiments were posted on Valentine's Hill, " one of those ridges which still form a distinguishing fea-

SOUVENIR. 51

ture in the topography of Westchester County: and at the time of which we write, the most beautiful of the high grounds extending northwardly as far as the White Plains, which were subsequently occupied by detachments of the American army, while the main body of that army was laboriously and painfully occupied in its famous retreat with its baggage and stores from the Heights of Harlem to the high grounds at the last mentioned place. And General Heath's division was posted in a line extending from Fort Independence to Valentine's Hill. It is said, also, that a line of entrenched encampments was formed along the high grounds on the western side of the Bronx River, from Valentine's Hill, on the south to Chatterton Hill, opposite the White Plains on the north." (Scharf's History of Westchester County, Vol. I. p. 414.)

General Washington established his headquarters on Valentine's Hill, just previous to the battle of White Plains. The information possessed by General Washington of the topography of the country, in the vicinity of Valentine Hill, was meagre, and he complains very much of the gentlemen of New York, from whom he had never been able to obtain a plan of the country. Colonel Putman in disguise reconnoitered the ground and sketched a map, giving the important features of the country and positions, but as will be seen from the map reproduced here, the ideas about the position of Valentine Hill with regard to Yonkers were very hazy and misleading. This section of Westchester County was the scene of the actions of the "Skinners" and the other guerrillas made famous in Cooper's novel, "The Spy." It abounds therefore in interesting associations.

PART II.

The Beginning of the History of the New Seminary.

I.

The Ceremony of the Blessing of the Corner-Stone of the New Seminary of St. Joseph.

On Pentecost Sunday, May 17th, 1891, His Grace, the Most Reverend Michael Augustine Corrigan, Archbishop of New York, in the presence of probably the largest concourse of Catholics ever seen in this country, blessed the corner-stone of the new Seminary Building, and also the corner-stone of the new Chapel.

The day itself was perfect, cool, and clear. In consequence nearly one hundred and fifty thousand people left their homes to witness the ceremony. Of these, owing to a lack of railroad accommodation, only about eighty thousand reached the grounds at Valentine Hill.

The Most Reverend P. J. Ryan, D. D., Archbishop of Philadelphia, delivered the following address, which was listened to with eager attention by a vast audience:

ARCHBISHOP RYAN'S ADDRESS.

"Confiding in Jesus Christ, we place this first stone in this foundation, in the name of the Father, and of the Son, and of the Holy Ghost, so that here may flourish true Faith, and the fear of God, and fraternal charity, and this place may be destined for prayer, for invoking and praising the name of the same Jesus Christ, Our Lord, Who lives and reigns God with the Father, and the Holy Ghost, forever and ever. Amen."-*Words of the Ceremonial of this occasion.*

Most Rev. Archbishop, Rt. Rev. and Rev. Prelates and Clergy, and Dear Brethren of the Laity:

I can expect to do little more this afternoon than to express aloud, and thus, perhaps, render more vivid and memorable, the thoughts and sentiments which must suggest themselves to your minds and hearts in view of the interest and importance of this occasion; an interest and importance which should not be confined to Catholics, but extend to all men, who desire the welfare and permanence of Christian society. To the Catholic this occasion has deep significance. He knows that Christianity is not merely a collection of ethical principles no matter how admirable, nor the fortuitous combination of persons under the names of Churches, who happen to agree on some leading doctrines of the Founder of the Christian religion, but that it is, and ever has been from its foundation, an organism, a Kingdom of God upon earth, compacted and fitly joined together, an organism of which the Christian Priesthood is an essential and inseparable portion. Christ and His Apostles formed the first Christian Seminary, and this Seminary has been perpetuated from century to century continuing in the world the divine priesthood of Our Lord with all its great powers, without which the Church cannot be conceived.

Again, it is well known that in proportion to the excellence of the intellectual and moral training in the Seminary shall naturally be the priests that come from its halls, and "as the priest, so the people." If we examine the history of the Church at various periods and in various countries, we shall find that the great body of the people were good or bad or indifferent according to the kind of priests that ministered to them. The priesthood should be, as the continued priesthood of Christ, "the salt of the earth," "the light of the world," and if it be not this, it becomes a curse to the world. If it be not for the resurrection it becomes for the fall of many.

Hence the immense importance of Seminary institutions for the welfare of all the children of the Church. This truth is particularly emphasized by the fact that when great reformers arose in the Church, they directed their first and most earnest endeavors towards the establishment of ecclesiastical Seminaries, the professors and pupils of which should be filled with the spirit of God. They went up to the mountain top, to the well spring of religious life and let the sweetening wood fall into the once bitter waters, and as these waters flowed downward and leaped over the rocks and formed the cataracts and swept by the great cities, bearing bread for the children of men, they retained the spiritual sweetness of their mountain heights.

At times, the Church, like her individual children, required reformation, not in doctrines and teaching, for these God preserves true and holy, but in the morals of priests and people. What

God has formed man should not dare to reform. As well attempt to improve the mechanism of the Heavens and change the natural laws of the earth, as reform God's work or the supernatural order. Hence the great mistake made by the so-called reformers of the sixteenth century. Had they attempted to reform, not God's work but man's work, not doctrines but morals, which sadly needed reform in priests and peoples, they might have done incalculable good. The doctrines were the same which had been believed in the primitive ages of Christianity, and with which and by which saints had been formed at the very time of the reformation. Moral not dogmatic reform was needed. This the great Council of Trent attempted and to a great extent effected. It was a reformation from within. And the Council directed its special attention to ecclesiastical seminaries.

"If," says Bishop Hefele, the historian, "the Catholic World has had for the last three hundred years a more learned, a more moral, and more pious priesthood than that which existed in almost every country, before the so-called Reformation, it is due to this decree of the Council of Trent, and to it, in this age, we owe our thanks." The Council directed that preparatory seminaries should be established for the younger aspirants to the ministry, and larger ones for the more advanced.

Few people advert to the long course of studies and training required for the priesthood of the Catholic Church. In two or three years a professional man may become a clergyman in some of the non-Catholic denominations, and if he please he can give up his ministerial calling, and return to his former profession. Not so, however, in the Catholic Church. In it, a priest once is a priest forever. The indelible mark of his priesthood is impressed on his soul. He cannot change. Hence, the immense importance of his training. He must have a desire for the state, an aptitude for the state, and sufficient virtue to preserve his innocence in this holy position. Because some were admitted into the sanctuary who possessed not these qualifications, great abuses crept in with them, and extended to the whole flock of Christ. Hence, the great reforming Council of Trent resolved to lay the axe to the root, and reform priesthood and people by reforming the seminaries, and making them all that they should be. The Council was justly persuaded that it was better to have fewer priests thoroughly trained, and filled with the spirit of sacerdotal piety, than many tepid or unworthy ones.

The priest is only the agent of God. Through him God ordinarily acts on his people, preaching and baptizing, and forgiving sins. But God has not abdicated His power to act directly on human souls, and it is infinitely better to leave such souls to God's direct action than to permit them to be scandalized by unworthy priests, who have ever been, and still are, the Church's greatest enemies—the salt that has lost its savor, and is fit only to be cast out and trodden under the feet of men.

But the Council was not satisfied with the personal sanctity of the candidates for the sacred ministry. The Fathers demanded that the studies in these seminaries should be of so high a standard that the Catholic priests should preserve their places as the great leaders of thought in the world. The priest was to be the model man, intellectually and morally, and he was to be formed for this exalted position in these retreats of learning and sanctity. St. Charles Borromeo was the first to carry out in all its details the great scheme for the establishment of well-regulated ecclesiastical seminaries. St. Vincent de Paul and M. Olier, the founder of the Sulpitians, in France, in 1650, continued the great work. The Sulpitians were instituted for the express purpose of conducting clerical seminaries, and the good they have done for ecclesiastical training, and through this for the Church, for priests and people, has been incalculable.

The Bishops who ruled this great diocese in the past felt the importance of a suitable ecclesiastical seminary. The history of their efforts in this direction is narrated in the souvenir pamphlet of this occasion, which renders unnecessary any detailed account of them by me.

Your devoted Archbishop is acting out the spirit and legislation of the Church and her reforming saints in the great Seminary about to be erected on this spot. Oh, what a future it shall have! Hundreds, even thousands, of young men in the very morning of life, in the spring-tide of existence, shall leave the great city yonder—leave human love and human ambition—and entering into the chapel, the future heart of this great institute, shall cry out in the inspired enthusiasm of their vocations: "We shall go in unto the altar of God, to God who rejoiceth our youth." "Send forth Thy light and Thy truth; they have led us and brought us to Thy holy hill and into Thy tabernacles." After years of solitude, prayer and study they shall go forth as the Apostles of Jesus Christ went forth on this Pentecost day, and entering again into the great city they shall proclaim, in words of fire, the holy truths that once converted the world, and which alone shall preserve it from moral destruction. Back to this retreat shall they come from time to time to renew the spirit of their exalted vocation, and to go forth, thus renewed, to continue their great work. The mission of this institution is thus eloquently described in the address of the old Seminary to the New, in the Souvenir:

> Here is the school of Christ—the upper room
> Where men shall learn to know the bud and bloom
> Of saintly lives; where Christ Himself shall teach.
> Illume the mind and wake the chords of speech
> Here men will dwell, to learn God's holy will,
> That He who built the Church must guide her still.
>
> Christ has not lied; this pompous world has need
> Of high inspiring word and god-like deed
> Of men who lift themselves above the clay
> And yearn to show their fellow men the way.
> Of men whose spotless souls are all aflame
> To teach the sweetness of the saving Name;
> Whose words and works, though like their Lord assailed,
> Prove that the gates of hell have not prevailed.

And for the non-Catholic, and even for the non-believer in Christianity itself, this occasion is not without interest. From a human standpoint alone the life mission of a Catholic priest is a glorious one. His love for and attention to the poor and suffering of our race; the great institutions of beneficence which the clergy of the Church have inaugurated and sustained in every part of the world; the truths so conservative of human society which the priest constantly inculcates; his respect for authority as of God's institution; his efforts for temperance and brotherly love; all the natural virtues which he fosters, ought to render the priest the best benefactor of his race, and the Seminary in which he has been formed for this glorious mission, an object of interest to every lover of his kind. But the plenitude of interest is found of course, in the Catholic heart. How magnificent and consoling is the scene before me. Here on this Pentecost day are represented nations as many and as diverse as those who thronged the streets of Jerusalem at the first Pentecost. On that day each man heard in his own tongue the wonderful works of God and the unity lost at Babel was restored to Jerusalem. A unity greater than this was produced by the Christian Church—a sacramental unity, all partaking of divine grace flowing from the seven channels from the heart of God—a governmental unity, all bowing in reverence and docility to the same pastoral authority, and above all and more marvellous than all, an intellectual unity, all believing the same doctrines. We need these unities in this age of discord. We need that the Pentecostal tongues of fire should descend again, and we begin to build the Cenacle where the future apostles shall await in holy prayer their descent.

O brethren, aid your holy and devoted Archbishop to accomplish what he and you commence to-day. This Seminary shall be the glory of his episcopate; and in that glory you shall be partakers; and if, as the Scriptures assure us, those who instruct many unto justice shall shine as stars for all eternity, surely they who contribute to the instructions of the priests and Bishops of the future shall not be left without their luminous reward in the firmament of God.

At the conclusion of the address, Archbishop Corrigan proceeded to bless the corner-stone of the chapel. He was assisted by the Right Reverend Bishops O'Farrell of Trenton, Wigger of Newark, Conroy of Curium, the Right Rev.

STONE QUARRY, SEMINARY GROUNDS.

Bishop Keane, Rector of the Catholic University at Washington, the Right Reverend Monsignor Preston, V. G., the Very Reverend Monsignors Farley and McDonnell, the Very Rev. Dr. Gabriels, President of St. Joseph's Seminary, Troy, the Very Rev. Dr. Hogan of the Catholic University, the Very Rev. Dr. Rex, President of St. John's Seminary, Brighton, the Very Rev. Dr. Magnien, President of St. Mary's Seminary, Baltimore, the Very Rev. Edward Allen, President of Mt. St. Mary's, Emmittsburg, the Very Rev. Fr. Campbell, S. J., Provincial of the Jesuits, the Very Rev. Fr. Wayrich. C.SS.R., the Very Rev. Fr. Spencer, O. P., the Very Rev. Rural Deans, McKenna of Westchester, O'Flynn of Saugerties, and Penny of Newburgh, and most of the clergy of the diocese.

Among the societies that took prominent part in the celebration were, the Society of St. Vincent de Paul, the Holy Name Societies, the Passion Sodality, the Bona Mors Confraternity, The Confraternity of the Holy Family, the Temperance Societies, the League of the Sacred Heart, the

Catholic Club, the Catholic Benevolent Legion, the Cadet Corps of St. John's College, Fordham, the Catholic Mutual Benefit Association, the Catholic Knights of America.

II.

The Opening of the New Seminary.

The First Mass.

On the morning of the 16th of July, 1896, the feast of our Lady of Mount Carmel, the first religious exercises were held within the walls of the new Seminary. At six o'clock, His Grace, the Most Rev. Archbishop, blessed the Sisters' Chapel, attended by his Secretary, Rev. James N. Connolly; Rev. Edward R. Dyer, S. S., Rector; Rev. Richard K. Wakeham, S. S., Treasurer, and Rev. William Livingston.

After the Chapel had been blessed, the Archbishop celebrated the first Mass in presence of those already named, and the following Sisters of Charity from Mount St. Vincent: Sister Marie Thérèse, Sister Marcella, Sister Jane de Chantal, Sister Maria Ambrose, Sister Mary Angelus, Sister Theresa Arthur, Sister Theresa Mary, Sister

Mary Lucy, and Sister Maria Genevieve. Sister Mary Lucina and Sister Mary Loyola were present at the second Mass, which was celebrated by Father Connolly, and served, as was the first Mass, by Mr. McLaughlin. The third Mass was celebrated by Father Livingston, the fourth by Father Dyer, and the fifth by Father Wakeham.

After breakfast a short recess was taken, and at 10:30 A. M. the Archbishop, attended as before, proceeded to bless the Sisters' House, the powerhouse, laundry, and bakery. There was no display on this occasion. Lovingly and reverently each room was sprinkled with holy-water, and the earnest prayer of the ritual repeated, invoking God's blessing upon every part of the house thus dedicated to a work so necessary and so holy.

The Dedication Ceremonies.

The vigil for the veneration of the Sacred Relics to be deposited in the altars was begun Sunday evening, August 9th, in the Sisters' Chapel, and was observed during the whole night.

On the morning of the 10th, at six o'clock, the Archbishop consecrated the main altar under the patronage of St. Joseph, placing there the Relics of St. Honoratus, St. Agatha, St. James the Greater and St. Vincent de Paul.

The Altar of the Sacred Heart was then consecrated, and the Relics of St. Severinus, St. Julia, St. Ambrose, and St. Alphonsus Liguori were placed therein.

The consecration of the Altar of the Assumption was reserved for the consecration of the Chapel proper, which will take place in 1898.

Immediately after the ceremonies, the Most Rev. Archbishop celebrated the first Mass on the high altar of the Chapel, and the Mass of Thanksgiving was celebrated on the same altar by the Archbishop's Secretary, Father Connolly. The first Mass celebrated at the Altar of the Sacred Heart was said by Rev. M. J. Lavelle, Rector of the Cathedral.

The eve of the dedication was deemed an opportune time for the blessing of the Seminary proper. Bishop McQuaid of Rochester, at the request of Archbishop Corrigan, performed this work as a labor of love. He blessed the main building, which is to be used by the Professors and students, leaving the Chapel to be solemnly blessed next morning by the Archbishop.

At six o'clock on the morning of the twelfth, the day was begun by a proper and patriotic celebration on the lawn in front of the Seminary. A magnificent American flag, twenty by thirty feet in size, and having the complete number of stars, was blessed by the Rev. James N. Connolly, assisted by Father Driscoll and Mr. McLaughlin. The three then raised the banner of liberty to the top of a large white pole, which stands near the southeastern wing of the building. Thus, under the protection of the great ensign, stands St. Joseph's Seminary, not needing any other name. There are no signs or tokens of *royalty* about the place, but there are, and there will continue to be, every sign and token of *loyalty* to the American flag and the American Constitution.

Promptly at ten o'clock the Archbishop, attended by Dean Lings of Yonkers and Dean Sweeney of Kingston, began the ceremony of blessing of the new house of the Lord, and as the priests marched around in procession robed in cassock and surplice, they found the Chapel a fair and gladdening sight. The paintings behind the high altar were illumined by electric lights concealed behind the pillars and arch of the apse. The sanctuary was a dream of golden glory, while the simple, chaste beauty of the mosaic floor, the richness of the oaken stalls, the splendor of the marbled columns, and the wondrous color harmonies of the stained glass windows, sent a thrill of exultation through the souls of those who love and appreciate the glory of the house of God.

When the ceremony of the blessing was finished, the procession for the Solemn Pontifical Mass entered the Chapel. His Eminence, Cardinal Satolli, was the celebrant, attended by Very Rev. Monsignor Joseph F. Mooney, V. G., as Assistant Priest, Rev. John Edwards and Rev. Charles H. Colton as Deacons of Honor, Rev. John J. Kean, Deacon, and Rev. Matthew A. Taylor, Subdeacon of the Mass. The Masters of Ceremonies were Rev. James N. Connolly, Rev. Wm. J. Guinon, D.D., and Mr. Wm. S. McLaughlin.

The Subdeacon of the Cross was Rev. Thomas M. O'Keefe. Rev. John J. McCabe was Censer Bearer; Rev. Henry O'Carroll, Incense Bearer; Rev. Luke J. Evers and Rev. Michael Walsh, Acolytes; Rev. James D. Lennon, Mitre Bearer; Rev. James P. O'Brien, Crozier Bearer; Rev. Arthur J. Kenny, Jr., Candle Bearer; Rev. P. J. Mahoney, D.D., Book Bearer, and Rev. Thos. F. Myhan, Master of Choir.

Seated in the Sanctuary were Bishop McQuaid of Rochester, Bishop Wigger of Newark, Bishop Ludden of Syracuse, Bishop Gabriels of Ogdensburg, Bishop McDonnell of Brooklyn, Bishop Burke of Albany, Bishop McFaul of Trenton, and the Archbishop, attended by Very Rev. Albert A. Lings, V. F., and Rev. Michael J. Lavelle. More than two hundred priests occupied the stalls, with a few laymen invited as special guests by reason of their great interest in the building of the Seminary.

About twenty priests acted as a special choir, and sang the Gregorian Mass under the direction of Rev. Anthony Lammel, whose ability as a musician has long been known and appreciated.

When the solemn services were finished, the Rt. Rev. John M. Farley, D.D., Auxiliary Bishop of New York, ascended the altar, and read the following cablegrams of blessing and congratulation.

The first was a blessing from the Pope, and was addressed to His Eminence, Cardinal Satolli: " The Holy Father, on the occasion of the blessing of the new Seminary of New York, congratulates the Most Rev. Archbishop, and from the fulness of his heart imparts to His Grace, to the students of the Seminary, and to all the clergy of the diocese, his apostolic benediction.

"M. CARDINAL RAMPOLLA."

Cardinal Ledochowski's communication was addressed to Archbishop Corrigan, and was as follows :

"I congratulate your Grace, and rejoice with you most sincerely, that through your zeal and energy a building so monumental and so useful for the training of the young clergy has been completed ; and far from the scene of your labors, I invoke from my heart the blessing of Heaven upon the work, and pray that the young priests who shall be educated in this Seminary, which is a perfect model of its kind, may become also perfect models of the Catholic priesthood.

"M. Cardinal Ledochowski."

After reading these documents Bishop Farley preached the following sermon, taking for his text the words:

"Wisdom hath built herself a house."

"It has passed into a proverb of two worlds, that the progress of the Church in the United States has no parallel in the history of Christendom. Be this said with all humility, and let us not take to ourselves the glory that belongs to another. 'If Paul plants and Apollo waters, it is God alone that giveth the increase.' Nowhere in this broad land has this progress of our holy faith been so marked as in this, our own great city and diocese.

"Only four-score years ago the first resident Bishop took possession of his See, and New York became a separate ecclesiastical jurisdiction.

"When one tries to realize the condition of the Catholics of New York eighty years ago, when

Bishop Connolly entered upon his episcopal office with two small churches all-sufficient for the total Catholic population of the city, with a few thousand souls scattered throughout the length and breadth of the States of New York and New Jersey, with scarcely a dozen priests to minister to the spiritual wants of all ; when one contrasts that state of things with what we see around us today, one is forced to say, surely ' the finger of God is here.'

" In the interval between this present day of grace and thanksgiving which has brought us here, and the coming of the first resident Bishop, there have been days that stand out as milestones along this path of progress,—days fraught with joy and happiness in the memory of many yet living. Nay, this whole wondrous history has all come to pass in the lifetime of our glorious reigning Sovereign Pontiff, Leo XIII.,— *quem Deus diu sospitem incolumenque conservet.*

" It was a joy to the hearts of all the people and clergy when the first twelve laborious years of Bishop Hughes' episcopate were crowned with the pallium, and he became the first Archbishop of New York. It was an epoch in the life of the Church when that great Archbishop, verging to the close of his illustrious career, laid the foundation of his own monument—the grand Cathedral of our city. It was a day never to be forgotten when we saw his wise and saintly successor stand forth ' a Prince of the Church, in the royal dye of empire and of martyrdom, a pledge to us from Rome of Rome's unwearied love, a token that the American hierarchy was firm in Apostolic faith and hope.' It was a day of virtuous pride and gratitude when the first American Cardinal dedicated to the service of the Most High the grandest cathedral ever raised to the honor and glory of God on this continent.

"It was a day full of hope and divinest promise when, five years ago, 100,000 of the faithful from all parts of this vast diocese, with their pastors at their head, at the invitation of their venerated Archbishop, gathered around this place to witness the planting of the tree under whose spreading shade we repose to-day, and of which for ages to come this diocese shall enjoy the consecrated fruit.

"What went that multitude out into that desert to see? They went to testify their loyalty to the head of this diocese, and their love for the holy priesthood. They saw in faith the multitudes of God's ministers, who should be taught and trained, dedicated to God's service here—priests destined to break the bread of life to them and their children and their children's children. They came to register their devotion to the grand cause of Christian education in its highest and holiest sense. They came to proclaim their faith in the fact that the hour had come to lay the foundations of the greatest ecclesiastical seminary on the continent, and that with the hour had come the man to carry that divine work to its most perfect completion. They came to pledge themselves to hold up his hands in this arduous undertaking,—the most important work for education and religion ever projected in this diocese. Who that witnessed that generous outpouring of loyalty could doubt that the work begun that day would lag for lack of liberal support?

"I have said that it was the most important work ever undertaken in the cause of faith and learning. For it was designed to make that provision for souls without which the Church would fail and fade from the earth. It was to do for the Church of our day what Christ was pleased to do in the beginning to ensure the success of His Divine plans, when He made choice of His Apostles. The chosen twelve were the first seminarians, and the three years spent at the feet of the Master by the lakes and on the mountain sides of Judea was their seminary life. These years of teaching by Christ's words and example had to precede the divine commission which all priests receive. Not until He had inured them to self-denial, to habits of meditation on things of heaven and eternity; until He had led them into the knowledge of the sacred mysteries of His holy doctrine; not until then did He say to them: 'Go, teach all nations, teaching them all things whatsoever I have commanded you.'

"Not until His last night on earth with them did He say to them: 'Do this in commemoration of

Me,' thus imparting to them the awful power of offering to the living God the sacrifice of His own divinity and humanity for the sins of men.

"Not until those first seminarians had the hatred and horror of sin burned into their souls, had learned and looked upon the mystery of sin in all its hideous deformity, in the crime of Calvary, did the Son of God say to them: 'Receive ye the Holy Ghost; whose sins you shall forgive they are forgiven them, and whose sins you shall retain they are retained.'

"Even so, brethren, to this day, and so it will be to the end, has the Church His spouse done and shall do in making choice of her ministers. Until she has moulded them, as far as poor human nature will allow, into other Christs by meditation on this highest model, until they have acquired such knowledge of sacred and profane things as their high mission and the times and circumstances demand, will the Church intrust to them a ministry not given to angels.

"Warned by the Apostle ' to impose not hands lightly on any man,' and remembering that none must assume to himself this sacred office unless called by God, as Aaron and the Apostles were, the Bishops of the Church in all ages, in whom alone resides the power of renewing and perpetuating the sacerdotal line, have held it to be the gravest responsibility of their office, to make choice of the most worthy to whom they may commit the powers and commission of the divine apostolate.

"And thus it came to pass that from the earliest ages of the Church the Bishops trained the candidates for the holy priesthood either under their own roof or in seminaries specially adapted for the purpose, but always under their own eye or under the direction of trusted, learned, and holy men. And whenever this wise provision was neglected or departed from, the priesthood deteriorated, learning languished, morals relaxed and evils unnumbered fell upon the Church.

"It was the multitude of such evils that led the Council of Trent to decree that wherever possible it was the duty of the Bishops to see that candidates for the holy ministry should be trained in diocesan seminaries under the very eye of the Bishops themselves.

"Hence we find that the holiest and most apostolic amongst the Bishops of modern times, like St. Charles Borromeo and St. Alphonsus Liguori, whose lives were full of almost superhuman labors and cares, gave their gravest thoughts and the greatest part of their time to the care of their young clergy in their seminaries. St. Alphonsus used to call his seminary 'the apple of his eye, the jewel of his diocese.' Nothing seemed too much if it related to the young clergy. ' All my clergy are my crown,' he said, 'but I depend most on the seminary to cultivate and make morality reign throughout the diocese.' And St. Charles Borromeo, whose princely private fortune and large ecclesiastical revenues were all too meagre to meet the desires of his charitable soul, gave more liberally to his seminaries than to any other of his works; even as one whom we all so revere has been the foremost amongst the benefactors who have built up this splendid institution. Look around you and say if this Chapel, his gift—the holy of holies of this sacred place—is not worthy of him who has taken St. Charles for his model!

"It has always been the ardent desire of the Bishops of this diocese to have a seminary of its own. As far back as the time of Bishop Dubois, when the resources of this diocese were hardly sufficient to provide the Sacraments for the faithful, when the churches were few and poor, and the people likewise, the holy Bishop undertook the building of a college and seminary at Nyack-on-the-Hudson. But an accident shortly reduced the place to ashes. His illustrious successor, the first Archbishop, after some years established the Seminary of St. Joseph at Fordham, which flourished for many years, and gave many noble and zealous clergy to the diocese of New York; amongst them the three late Vicars-General, Starrs, Quinn, and Preston. But for economic reasons it was found necessary for all the dioceses of the province to unite in one Provincial Seminary, which was established at Troy. There for a generation the clergy of New York were instructed and moulded under a body of learned and devoted priests, to whom this province and diocese must ever remain deeply grateful. For if this vast diocese, one of the largest and most important in the whole Church, with its 800,000 souls, is zealously and faithfully cared for from the centre of the metropolis to the remotest mountain mission ; if it is provided with spacious and handsome churches and schools and charitable institutions, it is after God and under direction of the Archbishops, mainly owing to the splendid body of priests, numbering to-day fully 90 per cent. of the clergy of the diocese, who have been so ably and efficiently trained and formed in St. Joseph's Seminary, Troy, which, full of years and of merits, having fulfilled its mission, has now passed away.

"The time had come for New York to have her own seminary within her own limits, as had been originally intended by the former Bishops of the diocese; a seminary so placed that it should be under the eye and immediate guidance of the head of the diocese. That the time was ripe for it is evidenced by the marvellous success that has attended the work from the moment of its inception. That within five years from the laying of the first stone, 'this monumental structure, the most perfect model of its kind,' as Cardinal Ledochowski calls it truly, should have reached completion, with only such a residue of debt as a brief space will wipe out, is something without precedent in the Church of this country.

"All know to whose energy and zeal this wondrous success is due. He took no rest or repose till it was accomplished. To him may be applied in this instance the words of Scripture: 'He vowed a vow to the God of Jacob: if I shall enter into the tabernacle of my house, if I shall go up to the bed in which I lie, if I shall give sleep to my eyes or slumber to my eyelids, or rest to my temples, until I find a place for the Lord, a tabernacle for the God of Jacob.' I know that I am violating the reserve which is peculiarly his when I speak thus; but I cannot on such an occasion suppress the expression of what I know to be the feelings of all here to-day.

"Your Grace, this must be for you one of the

most consoling days of your life. Your heart goes out in thanksgiving to Almighty God, without whose help 'they labor in vain who build,' that you have lived to see this day. Your illustrious predecessors in this See sighed to behold this day; they saw it in spirit and were glad. They knew it would come,—that God would provide the means and the man. They see it to-day from on high. As your anointed brow bowed down this morning, whilst the *gratias agimus tibi* ascended to heaven from the tongue of the Eminent Prince celebrant, and on the wings of the Church's glorious chant from the lips of the consecrated choir of priests, methought I saw—who could help thinking so?—amidst the just made perfect, the spirits of your eminent and illustrious predecessors in this See — McCloskey, Hughes, Dubois, and Connolly,—with the whole host of holy patrons of the churches and institutions of this diocese, take up that chant and repeat, '*gratias agimus Tibi, Domine Deus, Agnus Dei.*' Who can doubt that as they laid at the feet of the Lamb, this latest and greatest gift of a grateful clergy and people, this future home of piety and learning, who can doubt, I say, that these holy patrons and prelates united their prayers and pleadings with those that fill your heart and the hearts of all the prelates and priests and people here to-day, that the Eternal Father would pour out upon this Seminary and upon all who shall dwell therein, the fulness of His blessing; that the Great High-Priest may make intercession for those who are to be made after His likeness here; that they may be most perfect models; that the Holy Spirit may diffuse upon the souls of the young levites soon and for centuries to come, to fill these noble halls, His light and His grace; that as generation after generation of young priests go forth from these sacred precincts, they may bear away with them the fulness of His wisdom and understanding, and counsel and fortitude, and knowledge, and piety, and the fear of the Lord! That they may go and bring forth fruit, and that their fruit remain, to the honor and glory of God, to the salvation of souls, and to the lifting up of this our own belov-

PARTICIPANTS IN THE DEDICATION CEREMONIES, AUGUST 12, 1896.

ed country to still higher planes of truth and honor and national prosperity."

At the conclusion of the sermon, the Archbishop, in cope and mitre, standing before the high altar, intoned the *Te Deum*, and immediately the Bishops and Priests took up the strain. The glorious old anthem of praise and glory and gratitude rolled and echoed through the noble arches of the Chapel and soared aloft to God.

The Dedication Dinner.

At about one o'clock dinner was served in the large students' dining hall. There were no toast cards, nor was it intended that any number of speeches should be made. It was impossible, however, even though the heat was exceedingly oppressive, to let such an occasion pass without some expression of the gladness that beamed from the faces of all who were present. Towards the end of the dinner Archbishop Corrigan rose, amid a storm of hearty and sustained applause. His Grace waited till quiet was restored, and then spoke in his usual happy and gracefully-worded style.

The Archbishop's Speech.

"*Your Eminence, Right Reverend Bishops, Prelates, and Reverend Fathers:*—In consideration of the great heat of the day, a desire has been expressed, in an authoritative quarter, to dispense with the usual toasts, but we cannot allow this happy occasion to pass without proposing, as I shall do a moment later, at least one health, that will strike a responsive chord in the hearts of all present. Meanwhile, as in parentheses, permit me to give vent to the profound feelings of heartfelt gratitude with which all the incidents of this day overwhelm me. In particular, I beg to thank His Eminence, the representative of the Holy Father, for his great kindness in honoring this feast with his presence, and thus making us realize more vividly the loving benediction which His Holiness has been pleased to impart on this joyful occasion. Cordial thanks are also due to the venerable Bishops of this Province for their gracious attendance, notwithstanding other duties, distance, and uninviting weather, and for the kind felicitations which they have been good enough to express. But especially on this day of days, deep gratitude is tendered to those who have so nobly aided in this important work from its very foundation, the zealous and generous Clergy, and the no less devoted Laity of this diocese. Notwithstanding the hard times and the financial depression that have prevailed for the past five years, the living spring of charity has never ceased to flow ; nor was it found necessary to suspend the work, through lack of funds, even for a day. Signal gratitude is due to the gentlemen, both of the Clergy and Laity, who form the Committee of Ways and Means. They assisted in choosing this site, in approving the plans and contracts, in obtaining the necessary funds ; and from the very outset have given the benefit of their advice, their encouragement and support, and their experience. In the furnishing of the Seminary, the services of the Sisters of Charity have been invaluable ; and, in this connection, I cannot omit the untiring zeal of my secretary, Father Connolly, who has devoted months and months in looking after innumerable details as regards the construction and lighting of the building, the equipment of the chapel and sacristy, the health, the comfort, and the conveniences of the students.

" Permit me, in conclusion, to welcome to the diocese, and to commend most kindly to all present, the Sulpician Fathers who are to have charge of this institution. Thus far they are known to the majority of us only by reputation,—a reputation for earnest and sustained devotion to their work which was voiced so impressively on his deathbed by the illustrious Fenelon, when he declared: 'I know nothing in the Church of God more venerable or more apostolic than the Society of St. Sulpice.' It is safe to predict that the more thoroughly we know these reverend gentlemen, the greater will be our regard for them, our reverent esteem, and our admiration.

"And now, closing the parenthesis already long-drawn-out, permit me, your Eminence, Rt. Reverend and Reverend Brethren, to propose to you the health, the long life and happiness of our Holy Father, Pope Leo XIII. 'May the Lord preserve him, and give him life, and make him blessed upon the earth ; and deliver him not up to the will of his enemies!'

" I trust His Eminence, Cardinal Satolli, the revered representative of our Holy Father, will not refuse to say a few words."

Cardinal Satolli, on rising, was greeted with warm and enthusiastic applause. He said a few words in English by way of introduction, and then began in Latin an address which stirred the hearts of his hearers. Every gesture was eloquent, every word was rich in meaning, every sentence clear-cut and luminous. It is impossible to give in English an exact equivalent of the Latin original. The following, however, expresses quite fairly the substance of the Cardinal's address :

" *Most Rev. Archbishop, Rt. Rev. Bishops, and Rev. Fathers:* It is to me a source of unbounded delight to be present on this occasion as the representative of the Holy See. I have studied the progress of this vast Archdiocese of New York, and have noted its flourshing condition. The Holy Father also has given it most special attention, and knows it not only as the greatest in the United

States, but also as one of the foremost in the world. This marvellous building is but a fitting monument to the generosity of the clergy and people of this metropolis. All the self-sacrificing works of the former Bishops and Archbishops of this diocese have now reached their climax through the intelligence, the prudence, and the zeal of your present great Archbishop, whom I congratulate in the name of the Holy Father, and to whom in the same name, as well as in my own, I wish many years of continued wise and useful administration. This Seminary, grand in its achitectural design, is a type of the Archbishop's heart; and it is an evidence of the wonderful hold he has upon the love and the generosity of the clergy and people.

"Let us remember, however, at the same time, that though the magnificence of this material edifice, typifying as it does the magnificent grandeur of our holy Mother the Church, is something for which we must all be happy and grateful, there is also required, to make it fruitful unto greater good, the spiritual edifice, the true ecclesiastical spirit, without which all material splendor would

ST. JOSEPH'S SEMINARY, WEST VIEW.

be useless. The generosity shown in building this structure will soon be followed by a still higher generosity in the upbuilding of the minds of those who soon will enter these portals. Here, knowledge with virtue will thrive in the souls of the youthful candidates for the priesthood. Their united names will stand as the synonym and type of the very highest civilization. Knowledge in any people is vain unless virtue accompany it. No matter how perfect the material civilization of any nation may be, it is a false culture unless to progressive knowledge be added progressive virtue.

"This age, possibly more than any other, demands this companionship. And the Church demands it especially in her chosen representatives. She stands to-day as the apostle servant of Christ, in the midst of a world that hates her, and will hate her to the end. But she uses every legitimate means to attain her noble ends. And where they are not wrong, she has no hesitation in using even the weapons of the enemy. With the aid of the sound philosophy and theology which will here be taught, much will be accomplished against the errors of the day. Naturally associated as knowledge and virtue are, it has always been a sad experience for the Church and for humanity, when through any cause they have been dissevered. Consequently, I would urge that the very best philosophy and theology should always be taught here, in the very best possible manner. What is the best philosophy and theology? As St. Paul said, ' I am not ashamed of the Gospel,' so do I say: ' I am not ashamed to be a Thomist.' And among the many wonderful works of our Holy Father, Pope Leo XIII., there is none for which either he or the Church has reason to be more grateful, than his insistence upon the teaching of the philosophy and theology of St. Thomas. Cultivation of this absolutely sound system is the great desideratum of our age. We need not newness of theories; what we require is solid Christian doctrine. This is what has been provided for us by St. Thomas. And against the whole world I would defend it as the highest type of what the system of teaching truth should be. It gives full play to reason as well as to faith. It is analytical, and at the same time critical. It is profound, yet clear. It is broad, but incontrovertible. So powerful is its arrangement of facts, so correct its logic, so strong its arguments drawn from the inexhaustible fountains of reason and faith, that beyond all other systems it strengthens the mind, and makes men able, while contemplating the heavens, to also rule the earth. This is the quality of mind especially required in the priest of the present day. This is the happy mental condition our Holy Father, Leo XIII., expects the clergy of America to possess. He is the great propagator of the doctrines of St. Thomas, and no more pleasing news could reach the supreme Pontiff than that in the Church in America, whose future is to be so great, the Angelic Doctor will be assiduously and thoroughly studied. I wish the Seminary all possible prosperity and success. May it be like the good soil mentioned in the gospel, in which the best of seed will be sown, producing a generation of priests, who in their turn will produce and guide a nation of Catholics, the wonders of whose faith and virtue will be even greater than those of their fathers before them."

When the Cardinal ceased, Father Captier, Superior-General of the Sulpician Fathers, who was present on a visit from France, rose at the request of the Archbishop, and made an address in French. The venerable old man expressed his congratulations and his joy on such an auspicious beginning of a great work, and expressed his heartfelt thanks to the Archbishop for selecting the Sulpician fathers as guides and teachers for the future priests of the Archdiocese.

Bishop Gabriels of Ogdensburg then rose in response to repeated calls from the old students of Troy, and said:

"What is a day of joy to many of you, is, to not a few, an occasion of some sadness. The opening of St. Joseph's at Dunwoodie marks the end of a beloved institution, St. Joseph's of Troy. '*Ilium fuit*,' may be said of the old Seminary; happily it is not so with the glory of its sons. The glory of the Trojans is and will continue to be a living thing throughout this large continent. Wherever I travelled I found it known and honored. '*Quæ regio in terris non nostri plena laboris?*' In every part of this broad land the sons of St. Joseph's of Troy are spending themselves in labors for churches and institutions of all kinds.

"St. Joseph was in exile for many years. He is now called from Egypt to his own home in Nazareth. Let us bear in mind, however, that in Palestine as in Egypt, St. Joseph was the custodian of his Master, the model of the priest.

"One thing I wish to remark about the students of Troy, without presuming to say that they are more so than others: they are loyal to the Holy See. Our Lord said to Peter: '*Diligis me plus his?*' and he answered: 'Lord! Thou knowest that I love Thee!' So, too, if asked they could answer: Holy Father, you know that we love you. And I would ask His Eminence, the Apostolic Delegate, when he returns to Rome, there to benefit still more the American Church, to lay this fact at the feet of His Holiness, that there are in this Archdiocese seven hundred priests full of loyalty and love for him.

"To conclude, I wish to the successor of Troy,

the new Seminary of New York, a happiness which the former did not enjoy. It lasted only the space of one generation of priests. May the new Seminary last for generations and generations. I say, therefore, with all my heart, to the new St. Joseph's, '*Esto Perpetua!*'"

The old students of Troy applauded their former professor and President with hearty goodwill, and his expressions of love for the Holy Father and the Seminary were rapturously receeived.

A general call for the venerable Bishop of Rochester followed, and he rose with no unwilling heart.

" I am not a stranger here," he said, and a perfect whirlwind of applause emphasized the truth of that statement. " I am probably the oldest New York priest in this hall," he continued, " but I think too much of you to inflict anything more upon you than is necessary to express my congratulations to the Archbishop, the priests, and the people of New York on the completion of this Seminary, not of Dunwoodie, but of the greater

ST. JOSEPH'S SEMINARY. NORTH VIEW.

New York. Rev. Fathers, you have a Seminary the like of which does not exist anywhere else in the world. But it takes more than bricks and mortar to make a Seminary. You must have the men to teach, and you must have methods that are up to date. And just here let me remark that we have a Seminary in Rochester, neither so large nor so grand as this, which, in other things, is going to set you a pace that will make you bestir yourselves to keep up with. If you are in old ruts, you will have to get out of them. No old methods, a century behind the age, will do.

"You have a building here that is a wonder and a charm, and I thank God that a new spirit is showing itself in regard to Seminaries. Years ago it used to make me sad at heart to see magnificent structures in course of erection all over the country for orphan asylums and hospitals, while any old barn was thought good enough for the young levites, the men called by God to keep alive, in the hearts of the people, the very faith that made all our works of charity possible. But now in St. Joseph's of Dunwoodie and St. Bernard's of Rochester we have two buildings that challenge comparison with any in the world.

"As I said before, I am a New York priest, and an old one; therefore I feel at home among you. The first Bishop of New York baptized me, the second confirmed me, the third ordained me, and the fourth consecrated me."

There was a generous round of applause as Bishop McQuaid took his seat, and the guests retired, again to feast their eyes on the building, and express anew their satisfaction and delight with every detail of the magnificent structure.

A Short Financial History of the Seminary.

The Most Rev. Archbishop began the raising of funds for the building of the new Seminary, by inviting, in the month of June, 1892, a number of the Catholic gentlemen of this city to a meeting in the archiepiscopal residence. Twenty accepted the invitation. His Grace disclosed the project he had so deeply at heart in a neat and interesting speech. The result of his appeal was, that thirty-four thousand dollars were subscribed upon the spot.

His Grace next made it a point to speak to several of the prominent pastors, asking them to think out ways and means for obtaining the remainder of the fund. As the result of their suggestions, united with his own views, a meeting of all the pastors of the diocese was called in the Cathedral School Hall, on September 15, 1892. This gathering was presided over by His Grace, who proposed for the acceptance of all present, the following plan: That every parish in the diocese should for five years contribute the sum of two hundred dollars for each priest serving therein; that each city pastor should contribute personally one hundred dollars per annum; that each country pastor should donate seventy-five dollars a year; and that every assistant priest should subscribe fifty dollars for each of the designated five years. The proposition was unanimously accepted by those present, and on motion it was resolved that a committee of five be chosen to receive the monies, and to hold them until they should be transferred to His Grace. The committee chosen by the priests were the Rev. P. F. McSweeney, D.D., John F. Kearney, John Edwards.

On St. Joseph's day, 1893, a second meeting of the clergy was held, at which was read the report of the committee appointed by vote of the priests. It was found that more than sixty-five thousand dollars had been subscribed during the elapsed period.

In the following September, His Grace appointed a subsidiary committee of Ways and Means, consisting of the Rt. Rev. Mgr. Farley, Very Rev.

Jos. F. Mooney, V. G., Rev. Jas. J. Flood, Rev. M. A. Taylor, Rev. J. W. Power, Rev. M. J. Lavelle, Judge Daly, C. V. Fornes, James D. Lynch, John D. Crimmins, Jos. J. O'Donohue, Morgan J. O'Brien, C. Callahan, Jeremiah Fitzpatrick, and Wm. P. O'Connor. At their suggestion another meeting of lay gentlemen was called for the twenty-fifth of the same month. As the result of this gathering forty-five thousand dollars were added to the fund. It was furthermore resolved, as a consequence of this meeting, to establish a monthly newspaper, which should act as a means of keeping the project constantly and clearly before the public. Mr. John Mullaly was appointed the editor. The paper was styled simply, "The Seminary." It was published unremittingly every month until August, '96, and to its constant appeals to the generosity of the Catholic people, no small amount of the funds raised must be ascribed. Each year the clergy met in the Cathedral School Hall to hear reports, and they invariably had reason to be proud of the progress that had been made.

In January of the present year, the Most Rev. Archbishop, his Rt. Rev. Auxiliary, and Vicar-General Mooney, undertook to visit in turn on designated Sundays, all the parishes of the city of New York, with a view to presenting the Seminary fund personally before the people, and asking them in each church for an envelope collection. It was provided, also, that the country churches should be similarly visited by the Deans of their different districts. Through this new movement on the part of the ecclesiastical authorities, more than eighty-four thousand dollars have thus far been collected.

As the fund stands at the present moment, more than seven hundred thousand dollars have been paid into the hands of His Grace. No words are adequate to praise the priests and the people for the energy, the intelligence, and the generosity wherewith they have been able to subscribe the very large fund in such a short period of time, and in face of so many business embarrassments. The Catholic clergy and people have the proud satisfaction of knowing that they possess one of the finest Seminaries in the world, to which practically every single individual has contributed something.

The new St. Joseph's Seminary stands on Valentine Hill, a historic spot made memorable by Gen. Washington and his army during the war for independence. The site was chosen after long and mature consideration by His Grace, Archbishop Corrigan, aided by an able and zealous advisory committee, who examined numerous available places in the vicinity of New York, and selected this site for its beautiful and healthful location on the high plateau between the Sound and the Hudson River, easy of access from the City of New York, as well as from all other parts of the Archdiocese, and promising to be eventually one of the choicest locations of the Greater New York. The ground slopes from the building on all sides, assuring natural drainage as well as a beautiful landscape effect.

The property, which comprises over sixty acres of ground, was purchased in the beginning of the year 1890, and as an excellent building stone could be readily obtained on the premises, it was decided to erect the building of this stone, and soon after title was taken, excavations and quarrying of the building material were begun, so that by the end of that year, a large quantity of the fine rock-faced stone was prepared ready for use. In Spring, 1891, the foundations were prepared, and May 17, 1891, is the memorable day on which, in the presence of an immense concourse of dignitaries and people, the corner-stone of the new Seminary was laid. Since then work has been steadily progressing, and on August 12, 1896, we witnessed the dedication of the completed building, a monument to the grand and noble conception of an ideal Seminary, of His Grace, the Archbishop, and of the zeal and generosity of the priests and people of the diocese.

The architects, Wm. Schickel & Co., were entrusted by His Grace with the planning and the execution of this great work, and they have certainly succeeded in embodying the noble thoughts of its founder, in designing a building monumental in character, useful and well adapted in its ar-

STONE FROM QUARRY, SEMINARY GROUNDS.

rangements, and solid and substantial in construction, so that for ages the Seminary will stand as the cradle and home of the priesthood of the Archdiocese.

The hard rock found on the premises, suggested for the building a treatment in keeping with this material, and therefore the architects chose for the exterior a type of early Renaissance architecture, avoiding all carving or intricate work, and leaving to the natural beauty of the stone, and the general disposition and grouping of the masses, the effect to be attained in the design. For the interior, the Italian Renaissance of the end of the fifteenth century was adopted, being the style in which, after the revival of classic studies in the service of Christian art, many of the foremost ecclesiastical buildings of Europe have attained their refined and beautiful expressions.

The general disposition of the building is as follows: The front faces southeast, commanding a beautiful view of the Sound, and assuring sunlight to all rooms. The main building forms a hollow square open to the front, with a chapel as a central extension in the rear; and the refectory and domestic house form an additional group of buildings on the northeast. Eighy feet further away from them, are the boiler-house, electric light station, laundry, bakery, and other out-buildings.

The length of the main building is 360 feet, and the wings project 80 feet, while the dimensions of the chapel are about 40x130. The main entrance is emphasized by a massive portico with polished granite columns, and the centre portion of the building is surmounted by a grand cupola, the cross of which rises 150 feet above the ground, and is visible for many miles around.

The entire building is constructed absolutely fireproof, and even the use of iron has been reduced to a minimum. Fireproof tiles and blocks were employed throughout in the construction of the floors and ceilings, which are all vaulted, and the internal partitions are also all built of fireproof blocks. The high roofs, which give the building a most beautiful sky-line, are covered with copper and slate, and every effort has been made to insure durability and solidity in all parts of the building. All the stairs are constructed of tile arches, and the steps are of marble. The floors of the halls on the main floor are mosaic, and all bath-rooms, kitchens, toilet-rooms, etc., are tiled.

The building is heated by means of hot water, and the heating, ventilating, plumbing, etc., are all studied with special care to the comfort and well-being of the inmates of the house. The nicely-appointed bath-rooms deserve special mention.

The entire building is lighted by electricity supplied from two Edison dynamos.

The internal arrangement of the building is such that the basement contains large recreation rooms, bath-rooms, etc. On the main floor are located the entrance, vestibule, parlors, lecture halls, prayer halls, study rooms, chemical laboratory, physical cabinet, refectory, and all other public rooms, so that the entire floor is devoted to the common life of the seminarians, while in the three floors above this, they find their living apartments.

In the tower is a room containing the archives of the Archdiocese. The lecture halls are large and airy, well-lighted and well-ventilated rooms, equipped with all modern appliances for the studies.

The stairways and halls deserve special mention, as they are exceptionally large and well proportioned, and give the whole house a stately character. The central stair hall is adorned by four beautiful statues of St. Turibius, St. Rosa of Lima, Blessed Father Jogues, and Blessed Catherina Tegakwita.

The Seminary has accommodation for 160 students and twelve professors. Besides this, there are special suites of rooms for the Archbishop and Rector of the Seminary, and visitors. All rooms are bright and cheerful, and well furnished.

The upper story of the centre part of the building is occupied by the large library, an unusually fine room, fitted up with fireproof book-cases in two tiers, with handsome balconies and stairs, and on the main floor are large reading tables and desks, making this library a model of its kind.

THE CHAPEL, ST. JOSEPH'S SEMINARY.

The gem, however, of the whole Seminary, is the beautiful Chapel, the individual gift of His Grace, the Archbishop; and here the architects have created a most worthy, harmonious, and devotional crowning-point of the whole. All the arts have been called in requisition to aid in beautifying this sanctuary. The ceiling and dome are vaulted, and decorated in relief. The apse of the sanctuary, and the panels over the altars, are adorned with large paintings executed by Lamprecht; the windows, which represent a series of subjects appertaining to the Holy Sacrifice, were executed by Hardman, of London, and the beautiful statues are the work of Sibbel, the sculptor.

The altars are of Italian marble, and the stalls and other woodwork in the Chapel are executed in oak, and are, as well as the decoration, painting, mosaic and marble work, all in exquisite taste.

The domestic cares of the house are in the hands of the Sisters of Charity, and a special house has been built for the accommodation of the Sisters, which contains the kitchen, serving rooms, etc., all of which are fitted up with steam apparatus and cooking utensils of modern description, and in the most complete manner.

The boiler-house contains four large boilers for the water heating apparatus and steam. The engines, dynamos, pumps, etc., are located next to the boilers, and the laundry is above the machinery hall.

Between the Chapel and the west wing of the house, the terrace is enclosed, and forms a beautiful cloister, one of the principal attractions of the Seminary. On the easterly side, an open court corresponding to the cloister extends in the rear to a large esplanade, on which promising trees have been planted, so that shady, comfortable walks and recreation grounds will be ready in the near future.

The contracts for the work on the Seminary were executed by the firms hereinafter enumerated, and it should be said here that the quality of all the work is excellent, and the contractors deserve well-merited praise.

List of Contractors:

J. & G. Stewart,	Mason and Stone,	Yonkers, N. Y.
Jas. J. & F. P. Treanor,	Mason and Stone,	Hastings on Hudson, N. Y.
Ronald Taylor,	Granolithic,	156 Fifth Ave., N. Y.
Jeans & Taylor,	Carpenters (for window frames, etc.)	103 So. 5th Ave., N. Y.
Gustavino Fireproof Construction Co.,	Tile-arches,	New York.
John Neil,	Roofer,	434 W. 17th St., N. Y.
Grissler & Son,	Carpenters,	634 E. 17th St., N. Y.
Power Brothers,	Plasterers,	1764 Broadway, N. Y.
C. L. Eidlitz,	Electrician,	10 W. 23d St., N. Y.
R. L. Stewart,	Mason (for boiler house),	Yonkers, N. Y.
Barr, Reynolds & Co.,	Heating,	67 Dock St., Yonkers, N. Y.
O'Brien & Lavelle,	Gasfitting,	162 E. 28th St., N. Y.
A. G. Newman,	Bells & Tubes,	157 W. 29th St., N. Y.
Post & McCord,	Iron Work (boiler house),	289 Fourth Ave., N. Y.
T. J. Byrne,	Plumber,	377 Fourth Ave., N. Y.
R. Schroeder,	Tiling,	444 Greenwich St., N. Y.
Eschlimann & Pellarin,	Mosaic,	231 E. 28th St., N. Y.

Theis & Janssen,	Marble.	139th St., N. Y.
Klee Brothers,	Ornamental Plaster,	329 E. 40th St., N. Y.
Wm. H. Jackson & Co..	Iron for finish.	27 E. 17th St., N. Y.
A. B. & W. T. Westervelt,	Library Outfit,	102 Chambers St.. N. Y.
Duparquet, Huot & Moneuse Co..	Range and Cooking Utensils,	43 Wooster St., N. Y.
John Hardman & Co..	Windows,	London, England.
Mayer & Co.,	Stations.	47 Barclay St., N. Y.
Geo. P. Olcott.	Sewer. etc..	Orange, N. J.
Oakley & Keating,	Laundry,	40 Cortlandt St., N. Y.
C. E. Hall & Co.,	Marble Altars, etc.,	Boston, Mass.
W. Baumgarten & Co..	Stalls & Wooden Altars.	321 Fifth Ave.. N. Y.
J. V. Schaefer & Co..	Sacristy Outfit,	159 E. 88th St., N. Y.
Geo. Faulhaber.	Seats for Prayer Halls & Sisters' Chapel.	Cleveland, Ohio.
Tiffany Glass & Decorating Co.,	Decorating Chapel and Library,	333 Fourth Ave., N. Y.
Wm. Lamprecht.	Paintings for Chapel.	393 Sackett St., Brooklyn, N. Y.
J. Sibbel,	Statues.	214 E. 26th St., N. Y.
Howard Watch & Clock Co.,	Clock,	41 Maiden Lane, N. Y.
Otis Bros. & Co..	Elevator,	38 Park Row, N. Y.

The Old Seminary to the New.

The First Seminary.

.... "Then they returned to Jerusalem, from the mount that is called Olivet, which is nigh Jerusalem, within a Sabbath-day's journey. And when they were come in, they went up into an upper room, where abode Peter and John, James and Andrew, Philip and Thomas, Bartholomew and Matthew, James of Alpheus, and Simon Zelotes, and Jude *the brother* of James. All these were persevering with one mind in prayer with the women and Mary the mother of Jesus."—*The Acts of the Apostles*, Chapter I. 12, 13, 14.

I.

"All power in heaven and earth is given to me,"
Thus spake the Sovereign Lord in Galilee,
"Therefore I say to you: Go forth and teach
The nations of the earth. Baptize, and preach
What things soever I have spoken to you.
This is their law—bid them observe and do."[1]

* * * *

This was not all—the end was not as yet.
He spake again ; perhaps on Olivet
Before He blessed them and was lost to view ;
Perhaps within that chamber, where the few,
His chosen followers, sat down to eat—
His blood their drink, His sacred flesh their meat—
We may not say just where ; He spake again :
"Depart not from the city, but remain
Waiting the Promise. In that awful hour
The Father from on high will send you power
That going forth your lives and words may be
Throughout the world, a witness unto Me."[2]

* * * *

So when the cloud received him from their sight
They turned them to the city. Day and night,
Morning and evening found them waiting there

[1] Matthew xxviii. 18, 19, 20.   [2] Acts I. 4, 8.

SOUVENIR.

With Mary, Mother of the Lord, at prayer
  * * * *
The days wore on; the world was sunk in sin:
Foul crimes without and loathsome vice within.
Blood-purchased souls went forward to their doom.
Yet came no voice from out that upper room.
The Gospel bearers from the world had fled—
Christ and the preachers of his love were dead.

Dead to the sneering world, the sinful throng
That makes its pleasure judge 'twixt right and wrong—
Dead in the eyes of carnal minded men—
Dead—when around the world they should have been
Holding aloft the standard of the cross,
Saving the souls of men from endless loss—
Dead—Ah! the devil and his angels knew
What death was theirs. A death in which they grew
In grace and wisdom as the Lord had grown [1]
Who chose to dwell for thirty years unknown.

Dead to the world they were: with Christ they died
A living death, that sin might not abide [2]
Within their hearts. Dead, as the seeds that die
To spring towards heaven and bloom and fructify.

Such was their death—to sin and passion lost
Till dawned the morning of the Pentecost.

Then kneeling humbly with united mind,
Suddenly upon them, as a rushing wind
That filled the house, a sound from heaven came
Mighty in power, while the Spirit's flame
In parted tongues blazed on each bending head
And fired the souls of those accounted dead. [3]

Trembling they rose, who knew themselves so weak—
Trembling their human lips essayed to speak
Then, as they felt the Spirit of the Lord
Filling their wakened souls, with one accord
They rushed abroad, impatient to proclaim
The Gospel message and the Saviour's name.

II.

Spouse of the Christ! in every clime and age

[1] Luke II. 51, 52.   [2] Romans vi. 8, 11.   [3] Acts II. 1, 2, 3, 4.

SOUVENIR.

True to the Lord's command—thy heritage—
To teach the nations! on this Pentecost
Knowing what millions to their God are lost,
Angels to-day around the Father's throne
Fill Heaven with music for this corner-stone.

This mighty stone and sturdy rising walls
That bring such promise of the spacious halls
Where youth may learn, and pray and persevere
With Mary's influence and the angels near.

Where those who consecrate their lives to God
May learn the ways in which their Master trod.
May learn with glowing heart to read the Word
And hear him speak, as the Apostles heard.
Where love shall set their earnest hearts on fire
Until they blaze with one supreme desire
To cut, to burn, to cast away the dross
Of human weakness that would shirk the cross.

To love no flesh—to sever ties that bind
Making the body master of the mind—
To lay up treasures which no moths consume [1]
Absorbed at prayer, as in that upper room—
Living for Christ: with Him their daily bread
But lost to sin—with His Apostles dead.

Dead—but the Father and his angels hear
How speak these dead from fruitful year to year.
Low murmured prayers in ceaseless round ascend
For all the world, alike for foe and friend
Their hymns of joy arise as one sweet voice
While angels listen and the heavens rejoice,
Their chanted psalms, with love's appealing, swell,
Loosing for men the bonds of death and hell,
While voiceless love and supplication reach
Sublimer heights than ever human speech.

Such is the life these new Apostles lead
Bound to their Lord in every word and deed.
For them the banquet of his love is spread
For Him they live, though men account them dead.
Dead—Aye the devil and his angels know
What death is theirs. A death in which they grow
In grace and wisdom, till the wakening hour

[1] Matthew VI. 24.

SOUVENIR.

Bids them arise in God's almighty power.
Bids them go forth to preach for sodden ears
And bear, as bore their Lord, the coward sneers
Of those who lead the world, and walk abroad
Casting their spittle on the Church of God.
Bids them go forth, to bless, and touch, and heal,
And live such lives as force the world to feel
The power they exercise.
      Despite the boast.
That men no longer need the Holy Ghost
Vice reigns triumphant in her haunts of shame
And earth has still her deaf and blind and lame.
The Saviour speaks—men hear but human cries ;
The light streams downward —' tis' for sightless eyes;
He bids them walk—the passion palsied limb
Can bear no toil along the road with Him.
What power on earth can bid the palsied rise,
Or give God's light to error darkened eyes?
Where is the voice to raise the drooping head
Open the grave and vivify the dead ?—
Who can the innocence of youth restore;
Bid sinners go in peace and sin no more ? (¹)
Who can proclaim the love of Christ for men,
Turning their thoughts from earth to heaven again
Bringing back souls the world had long enticed ?—
Who, but Apostles from the school of Christ.

Here is the school of Christ—the upper room—
Where men shall learn to know the bud and bloom
Of saintly lives; where Christ Himself shall teach.
Illume the mind and wake the chords of speech
Here men will dwell, to learn God's holy will,
That He who built the church must guide her still.

Christ has not lied; this pompous world has need
Of high inspiring word and god-like deed
Of men who lift themselves above the clay
And yearn to show their fellow men the way.
Of men whose spotless souls are all aflame
To teach the sweetness of the saving Name ;
Whose words and works, though like their Lord assailed,
Prove that the gates of hell have not prevailed. (²)
     WILLIAM LIVINGSTON.

John VIII. 11.   ² Matthew XVI. 18.

Valentine Hill.

WILLIAM LIVINGSTON.

Before the Battle of White Plains, Valentine Hill was occupied by detachments of the American Army. There, also, about a stone's throw from the New Seminary, Washington established his headquarters.

1776.

Here on this hill, in the olden days,
    When veins ran warm with a patriot fire,
They stood in the ranks, their hearts ablaze,
    Shoulder to shoulder, son and sire.

And the virgin land they loved so well
    Was flushed with the rich, red blood they gave;
She rose in strength as her heroes fell,
    And to give her power they sought the grave.

Some of their forms are carved in stone,
    Their names are clothed with a nation's pride,
And thousands sank to their death unknown;
    For love they struggled, for love they died.

We honor them all, and we love the fields
    These resolute soldier martyrs trod;
And the seed they planted this harvest yields —
    The road of sacrifice leads to God.

1896.

Here on this hill, in these golden days,
    Their faces glowing with voiceless joy,
They stand prepared for the coming frays,
    Shoulder to shoulder, man and boy.

They bring to the famished, heavenly bread,
    That the souls of men may be fair and clean—
The world hears not their marching tread,
    And their banner floats to the breeze unseen.

But the sin-enslaved cry aloud for aid,
    And the spirits of evil hear and pause—
There never was yet a priest afraid
    To shed his blood in the Master's cause.

Some of their names will live for men;
    Thousands will rest 'neath a nameless sod;
They die that the dead may live again,
    For the road of sacrifice leads to God.

Appendix I.

We append a copy of the circular issued to the Catholics of New York by the Committee of Arrangements. In order to show the cosmopolitan character of this diocese, we add the translations that were made of the circular issued by the Committee of Arrangements.

Laying of the Corner=Stone of the New Seminary of St. Joseph.

AT VALENTINE HILL, NEAR DUNWOODIE STATION,

N. Y. CITY AND NORTHERN R. R.

Sunday, May 17th, at 3 P. M.

ARCHBISHOP'S HOUSE, 452 MADISON AVE.,

New York, April 25, 1891.

To the Catholic people of the Archdiocese of New York:

His Grace, the Most Reverend Archbishop, invites all the Catholics of the Diocese to be present at the blessing of the corner-stone of the new Seminary of St. Joseph, on Sunday, May 17th, at three P. M., at Valentine Hill, near Dunwoodie Station, on the New York and Northern R. R. The solemn ceremony will be conducted by His Grace, and the eloquent and learned Archbishop Ryan, of Philadelphia, will deliver the address. All the Catholic Societies of this Diocese have been officially invited to participate in the celebration. Since the laying of the corner-stone of our beautiful Cathedral, no event has been more important for the welfare of this Diocese than the beginning of the new diocesan Seminary. For many years our priests have been educated at the Provincial Seminary at Troy. Owing to the inconvenience of the location for both Bishop and Priests, it has been deemed opportune to carry out the suggestions and monitions of the holy Council of Trent, and build within the limits of our Diocese a Seminary that shall be under the immediate supervision of the Bishop, and accessible to the Clergy. A beautiful site has been secured at Valentine Hill, in the town of Yonkers, two miles from the northern limits of the City of New York, and it is proposed to erect thereon a building that shall cost half a million dollars. Our people understand the importance and the necessity of a holy and learned Priesthood, for the Priesthood is the source of the people's spiritual life. Consequently Catholics throughout the world love to see aspirants for the Sacred Ministry properly trained for their high vocation, and have at all times been distinguished for their generosity in furnishing their priests with the best education and the best care that their circumstances would permit. The laity of this diocese have not been wanting in this noble spirit. We appeal to them, therefore, to aid their priests in making this celebration worthy of themselves, of the great institution it inaugurates, and of our devoted chief Pastor, whose crowning glory it shall be to have left a Seminary that shall provide this vast diocese with learned and holy priests to supply the places of those who in the course of years must inevitably pass away. By their presence on this noteworthy occasion, our people will give public testimony of their interest in the work which so nearly concerns their own spiritual welfare.

With the approbation of His Grace the Most Reverend Archbishop, and with the consent of the Reverend Rectors of the different Parishes, this circular has been prepared for distribution under the direction of the undersigned Committee of Arrangements, appointed by the Most Reverend Archbishop to supervise this important ceremony.

Very Rev. Mgr. John M. Farley, *Chairman*.

Very Rev. Edw. McKenna, V.F., Very Rev. D. P. O'Flynn, V. F.,
Very. Rev. Wm. L. Penny, V. F., Rev John F. Kearney,
Rev. James W. Power, Rev. John A. Gleeson.
Rev. Albert A. Lings, Rev. Nicholas J. Hughes,
Rev. James J. Flood. Rev. Charles R. Corley,
Rev. M. J. Lavelle, Rev. N. N. McKinnon, S. J.
Rev. Andrew Ziegler, C. SS. R.

Grundsteinlegung

für das neue St. Joseph's Seminar zu Valentine's Hill, bei Dunwoodie Station, New-York City und Northern R. R., Sonntag, den 17ten Mai, 3 Uhr Nachmittags.
Palast des Erzbischofs, 452 Madison Avenue.

———

New-York, den 25ten April, 1891.

An die Katholiken des Erzbisthums New-York:

Seine Gnaden, der hochwürdigste Herr Erzbischof ladet hiermit alle Katholiken der Diöcese ein, bei der Grundsteinlegung für das neue St. Joseph's Seminar, am Sonntag den 17ten Mai, um 3 Uhr Nachmittags, zu Valentine's Hill, bei Dunwoodie Station an der N. Y. und N. R. R. zu erscheinen.

Seine Gnaden wird die feierliche Zeremonie vornehmen, und der beredte Erzbischof Ryan von Philadelphia wird die Anrede halten.

Alle Gesellschaften dieser Diöcese sind offiziell eingeladen, an der Feier theilzunehmen.

Seit der Grundsteinlegung unserer schönen Kathedrale hat sich nichts ereignet, das für die Wohlfahrt dieser Erzdiöcese wichtiger wäre, als der Anfang zu diesem neuen Seminar. Viele Jahre lang sind unsere Priester in dem Kreis=Seminar zu Troy herangebildet worden. Die Unbequemlichkeit der Lage für den Erzbischof sowohl als für die Priester hat es räthlich erscheinen lassen, die Empfehlungen und Rathschläge des Heiligen Konzils von Trient auszuführen, und innerhalb der Gränzen der Stadt New=York ein Seminar zu bauen, welches unter der unmittelbaren Aufsicht des Erzbischofs stehe und dem Klerus zugänglich sei. Deßhalb wurde ein schöner Bauplatz zu Valentin's Hill, bei der Stadt Yonkers, zwei Meilen von der nördlichen Gränze der Stadt New=York erworben, und man beabsichtigt darauf ein Gebäude zu errichten, das eine halbe Million Dollars kosten soll.

Jeder Katholik weiß, wie nothwendig und wichtig tugendhafte und gelehrte Priester sind für das geistige Wohl des Volkes.

Die Katholiken in der ganzen Welt sehen es daher gerne, daß die Kandidaten für den h. Priesterstand zu ihrem hohen Berufe wohl vorbereitet werden, und sind so freigebig, als es möglich ist, um ihren Priestern die beste Erziehung und Pflege zu verschaffen.

Auch den Katholiken der Erzdiöcese New=York hat diese

edle Freigebigkeit nie gefehlt. Wir wenden uns daher an Alle mit der Bitte, bei dieser großen Feierlichkeit zu erscheinen und ihr Scherflein beizutragen zum Seminar, das der Stolz des hochwürdigsten Erzbischofs und der ganzen Erzdiöcese sein, und heilige und tüchtiger Priester liefern wird, welche die Stellen der Dahingeschiedenen einnehmen werden. Durch ihre Gegenwart bei dieser feierlichen Gelegenheit werden unsere Glaubensgenossen öffentliches Zeugniß ablegen von ihrem Antheilnehmen an dem Werke, das die Wohlfahrt ihrer Seele so nahe angeht.

Dieses Circular ist mit der Genehmigung Seiner Gnaden des hochwürdigsten Erzbischofs und mit der Zustimmung der hochwürdigen Rektoren der verschiedenen Distrikte erlassen worden, um durch das unterzeichnete Fest-Committee, welches von dem hochwürdigsten H. Erzbischof zur Regelung dieser hochwichtigen Zeremonie ernannt worden ist, unter das Volk verbreitet zu werden.

Very Rev. Mgr. John M. Farley, Chairman.
Very Rev. Edw. Mc. Kenna, V. F.
Very Rev. Denis P. O'Flynn, V. F.
Very Rev. Wm. Y. Penny, V. F.
Rev. John F. Kearney.
Rev. James W. Power.
Rev. John A. Gleeson.
Rev. Albert A. Lings.

Rev. Nicholas J. Hughes.
Rev. James J. Flood.
Rev. Charles R. Corley.
Rev. M. J. Lavelle.
Rev. N. N. McKinnon S. J.
Rev. Andreas Ziegler, C. SS. R.

LA PRIMA PIETRA DEL NUOVO SEMINARIO DI SAN GIUSEPPE
NELL' ARCIDIOCESI DI NUOVA YORK, AL COLLE
VALENTINO PRESSO LA STAZIONE DUNWOODIE,
della ferrovia New York and Northern.

DOMENICA 17 DI MAGGIO ALL 3 POMERIDIANE,

DAL PALAZZO ARCIVESCOVILE,

452 MADISON AVENUE,

NEW YORK 25 DI APRILE, 1891.

Al popolo Cattolico dell' Arcidiocesi di Nuova York:

Sua Eccellenza il Reverendissimo Arcivescovo invita tutti i Cattolici della diocesi ad esser presenti alla posizione della prima pietra del nuovo Seminario di San Giuseppe nella Domenica 17 di Maggio alle 3 pomeridiane nel colle Valentino, presso la stazione Dunwoodie, della ferrovia New York and Northern. La solenne ceremonia sarà compiuta da sua Eccellenza; e l'eloquente ed erudito Arcivescovo di Filadelfia, Mgr. Ryan terrà un discorso. Tutte le società Cattoliche di questa diocesi sono state ufficialmente invitate a prender parte alla cerimonia. Dalla posizione della prima pietra della nostra bellissima Cattedrale nessun fatto fu tanto importante per il benessere di questa diocesi quanto l'impresa del nuovo Seminario diocesano. Da molti anni i nostri sacerdoti sono stati educati nel Seminario Provinciale a Troy. Ma a causa della inconvenienza della località per i vescovi e per i sacerdoti, fu giudicato opportuno, per effettuare i suggerimenti e i consigli del santo Concilio di Trento, fabbricare nei limiti della diocesi di Nuova York un Seminario che sarà soggetto all'immediata vigilanza del vescovo e accessibile al clero.

Un luogo ameno è stato acquistato nel colle Valentino nella città di Yonkers, due miglia dai limiti nordici della città di Nuova York, e si è determinato innalzarvi un edificio che importerà mezzo milione di dollari.

Il nostro popolo comprende l'importanza e la necessità d'un clero pio e dotto, perché il sacerdozio è la fonte della vita spirituale del popolo. Onde giustamente i cattolici di ciascun paese amano vedere gli aspiranti al sacro ministero rettamente istituiti nella loro alta vocazione, e mai sempre si distinsero per la loro generosità nel provedere i loro sacerdoti con ottima educazione con ottime cure per quanto le loro circostanze lo permisero.

Il laicato di questa diocesi non venne mai meno a questo nobile spirito. Noi adunque facciamo appello ad esso per ajutare i loro sacerdoti acciò rendano questa cerimonia degna di loro stessi e della grande instituzione che si va a inaugurare: anzi di far si che ciò dia occasione ad una dimostrazione di sincera lealtá al loro amato pastore, al quale sará corona di gloria l'aver lasciato un Seminario che provvederá questa vasta diocesi di un clero, pio e dotto, per supplire a quei posti che nel corso degli anni rimaranno vacanti.

Colla sua presenza in questa occasione notevolissima il nostro popolo dará publica testimonianza del loro interesse nell'opera che così prossimamente concerne il loro proprio spirituale vantaggio.

Colla approvazione di sua Eccellenza il Reverendissimo Arcivescovo e col consenso dei Reverendi Rettori delle differenti parrocchie, questa circolare é stata preparata per la distribuzione dal sottoscritto comitato regolatore, nominato dal Reverendissimo Arcivescovo per disporre questa importante ceremonia.

Il Reverendissimo Monsignor J. M. Farley.
Il Molto Rev. Ed. McKenna, V.F., Il Molto Rev. D. P. O'Flynn V. F.
"   "   William L. Penny, V.F., Il Rev. John F. Kearney,
Il Rev. James W Power,   John A. Gleeson,
"   "   Albert A. Lings,   "   "   Nicholas J. Hughes,
"   "   James J. Flood,   "   "   Charles R. Corley,
"   "   M. J. Lavelle,   "   "   N. N. McKinnon, S. J.,
        Rev. Andrea Ziegler, C. SS. R.

POSE DE LA PREMIÈRE PIERRE DU NOUVEAU SÉMINAIRE DE ST. JOSEPH, À VALENTINE HILL, PRÈS LA STATION DE DUNWOODIE, CHEMIN DE FER DE NEW YORK ET DU NORD.

DIMANCHE 17 MAI À 3 HEURES DE L'APRÈS MIDI.

ARCHEVÊCHÉ 452 MADISON AVENUE,

NEW YORK, 25 AVRIL, 1891.

Aux Catholiques du Diocèse de New York :

Sa grandeur Monseigneur l'Archevêque invite tous les catholiques du diocèse à la pose et bénédiction de la première pierre du nouveau Séminaire de St. Joseph, le Dimanche, 17 Mai, à trois heures de l'après-midi à Valentine Hill, près la station de Dunwoodie, sur le chemin de fer de New York et du Nord. La solennité sera présidée par sa Grandeur, et Monseigneur Ryan l'éloquent et savant Archevêque de Philadelphie délivrera l'adresse.

Toutes les Sociétés Catholiques du diocèse ont été officiellement invitées à prendre part à cette solennité.

La fondation d'un nouveau Seminaire Diocesan peut, à juste titre, être regardée comme l'évenement le plus importante et le plus digne d'être enregistré dans les annales religieuses de ce diocese depuis la pose de la première pierre de nôtre magnifique Cathédrale. Pendant plusieurs années nos prêtres ont été instruits au Séminaire Provincial de Troy. Vu l'inconvénient de la localité pour les Evêques et les prêtres il a été reconnu opportun de repondre les suggestions et exhortations du Concile de Trente, et de bâtir dans les limites du diocèse de New York un Séminaire qui sera sous l'immédiate surveillance de l'Evêque et accessible au clergé.

Un ravissant site a été assuré à Valentine Hill dans la ville de Yonkers, situé à deux milles des limites Nord de la ville de New York où l'on se proposé d'ériger un bâtiment dont le prix sera d'un demi million de dollars.

Les fidèles comprennent l'importance et la nécessité d'un saint et savant clergé, le sacerdoce étant la source de leur vie spirituelle. Aussi les Catholiques à travers le monde aiment à voir les aspirants au Sacré ministère bien dirigés dans leur haute vocation, et pour cela ils se sont distingués de tout temps par leur générosité à fournir à leurs prêtres la meilleure education et la meilleure direction possible. Les laïques de ce diocèse non't pas failli dans ce noble ministere.

Nous faisons appel à leur bienveillance afin qu'ils se joignent à leurs prêtres pour rendre cette célébration digne d'euxmêmes, digne de la grande institution qu'ils inaugurent et digne de notre devoué Pasteur en Chef, dont la plus haute gloire sera de laisser un Séminaire qui fournira à ce vaste diocèse de savants et saints prêtres pour remplacer ceux qui dans le cours des années doivent inévitablement nous quitter.

Par leur présence dans cette importante circonstance les fidèles donneront une preuve publique de leur interêt dans ce travail qui touche de si près à leur bien-être spirituel.

Avec l'approbation de sa Grandeur Monseigneur

l'Archevêque et le consentement des Révérends Curés des differentes paroisses cette circulaire a été préparée pour être distribuée par le soussigné Comité d'arrangement, nommé par sa Grandeur l'Archevêque pour présider cette importante cérémonie.

      Very Rev. Mgr. John M. Farley, *Chairman.*
Very Rev. Ewd. McKenna. V. F., Very Rev. Denis P. O'Flynn, V.F.
Very Rev. Wm. L. Penny, V Rev. John F. Kearney,
Rev. James W. Power,   Rev. John A. Gleeson.
Rev. Albert A. Lings,   Rev. Nicholas J. Hughes,
Rev. James J. Flood   Rev. Charles R. Corley,
Rev. M. J. Lavelle.   Rev. N. N. McKinnon, S. J.
     Rev. Andrew Ziegler, C. SS. R.

Položení základního kamene nového semináře sv. Josefa na Valentine's Hill, blízko Dunwoodie Station na New Yorské a Severní žel. dráze (N. Y. City and Northern R. R.) v neděli, dne 17. května 1891, ve 3 hod. odp.

Z rezidence nejd. p. arcibiskupa,
452 Madison Ave.
New York, dne 25. dubna 1891.

Katolickému obecenstvu arcidiecese Newyorské:

Jeho Milosť nejd. p. Arcibiskup tímto zve všecky katolíky diecese, by se dostavili k slavnému svěcení základního kamene nového semináře sv. Josefa, v neděli, dne 17. května, ve 3 hod. odpoledne, na Valentine's Hill, blízko Dunwoodie Station (New York and Northern R. R.). Svěcení bude konati Jeho Milosť, a kázati bude výmluvností a učeností slovutný arcibiskup filadelfský, nejd. p. Ryan. Všecky katolické spolky pozvány byly, aby slavnosti te se súčastnily. Od položení základního kamene krásné naši katedrály nebyla událosť důležitější pro duchovní blaho diecese, než začátek toho nového biskupského semináře. Kněží naši až dosavad byli vychováni v provincialním semináři Trojském. Ale poloha toho ústavu nebyla příhodna ani pro arcibiskupa, ani pro duchovenstvo a proto uznáno bylo za dobré, vyhověti návrhu a přání sv. sněmu tridentského, a stavěti seminář v samé diecesi pod bezprostředním dozorem biskupa a přístupnější vel. duchovenstvu. Tím úmyslem zakoupeny byly krásné pozemky na Valentine's Hill v Yonkers, dvě míle od severních hranic města New Yorku, a usneŠeno stavěti velkolepou budovu za pět set tisíc dollarů ($500.000). Lid náš dobře pochopuje důležitosť a potřebnosť zbožného a učeného kněžstva, neboť od kněžích závisí duchovní život lidstva. Proto také katolický lid po celém světě chce, aby čekanci tohoto svatého úřadu patřičně byli připraveni, a ze všech časů štědrostí se vyznamenával, když se jednalo o náležité vyučování a vychování kněžstva. I katolíci naši diecesi v obětavosti nezustávali pozadu. Proto i nyni k nim se obracíme s prosbou, aby duchovenstvu nápomocni byli, a slavnosť tu učinili hodnou katolického občanstva, hodnou velkolepého ústavu, kterýž má zahájiti a hodnou milovaného našeho nejvyššího Pastýře, jemuž bude k největší cti a slávě, že vystavěl seminář ve kterém pro velkou diecesi tu zbožní, učení kněži budou vychováni, způsobilí zaujmouti místa těch, kdož dřív aneb později odstoupiti musí. Přítomností svou při slavnosti té lid náš veřejně dosvědčí, jak mu na srdci leží dílo duchovního blaha jeho tak velmi se týkající. Se svolením Jeho Milosti, nejd. pana arcibiskupa, a s dovolením vel. správců rozličných osad, oběžník ten byl připraven k rozdání od nížepsaného pořádacího výboru, jenž Jeho Milost k vedení slavnosti ustanovila.

DE EERSTE STEEN
Van Het Nieuw St. Jozef Seminarie,
op Valentine Heuvel, by de statie van Dunwoodie, stad New York en Noordsche spoorweg.

Zondag, 17en Mei, om 3 uur namiddag. Aartsbisschoppelyk paleis, 452, Madison Avenue.

New York, 25 April, 1891.

Aan de Katholieken van het aartsbisdom New York.

Zyne doorluchtige hoogwaardigheid de Aartsbisschop noodigt al de katholieken van het bisdom uit om tegenwoordig te zyn by het wyden van den eersten steen van het nieuw seminarie van St. Jozef, Zondag den 17en Mai, om 3 uur namiddag, op Valentine Heuvel, naby de Dunwoodie statie; langs den New York en Noordschen spoorweg. De plechtige ceremonie zal door zyne Hoogwaardigheid voorgezeten worden, en de welsprekende en geleerde heer Aartsbisschop Ryan van Philadelphia zal de redevoering uitspreken. Al de katholieke genootschappen van dit bisdom zyn officieel uitgenoodigd geworden de viering by te wonen. Sedert het leggen van den eersten steen onzer schoone hoofdkerk is geene gebeurtenis belangryker geweest voor de welvaart van dit bisdom dan het begin van het nieuw bisschoppelyk seminarie. Gedurende veel jaren zyn onze priesters gekweekt geworden in het Provinciaal seminarie van Troy. Doch uit rede van het ongemak der ligging voor den Bisschop en de priesters is het nuttig geoordeelt geworden de aanbeveling en de voorschrift uit te voeren van het heilig Concilie van Trenten en in de grenzen van ons bisdom een seminarie te bouwen hetwelk onder de onmiddelbare overzicht van den Bisschop zal staan en voor de geestelykheid gemakkelyk zal zyn om te bezoeken. Een schoone grond is daarvoor aangekocht geworden op Valentine Heuvel, in et kanton van Yonkers, twee mylen van de noordelyke grenzen der stad New York, en men heeft voorgenomen daar een gebouw op te richten dat een half millioen dollars zal kosten. Onze geloovigen beseffen het belang en de noodwendigheid van eene heilige en geleerde geestelykheid, want de priesters zyn de bron van het geestelyk leven des volks. By gevolg zien de katholieken der gansche wereld geern de kandidaten van het heilig ministerie goed onderwyzen voor hun hoog beroep, en in alle tyden hebben zy zich onderscheiden door hunne orygevigheid om aan hunne priesters de beste opvoeding en de beste zorg te verschaffen welke hun toestand hun toeliet. De wereldlyken dezes bisdoms zyn niet ten achter gebleven in deze edele geests gesteltenis. Wy roepen daarom op hen om hunne priesters te helpen deza viering weerdig te maken van van henzelven, van het groot gesticht hetwelk zy inhuldigt, en van onzen zelfopofferenden Opperherder, wiens kroonende glorie het zal zyn van een seminarie nagelaten te hebben dat dit uitgestrekt bisdom zal voorzien met geleerde en heilige priesters die de plaats zullen nemen dergene welke in den loop der jaren onvermydelyk moeten verdwynen. Door hunne tegenwoordigheid by deze merkbare gelegenheid zullen onze katholieken eene openbare getuigenis geven van hun belang in het werk hetwelk van zoo naby hun eigen geestelyk welzyn gemaakt.

Met de goedkeuring van Zyne doorluchtige Hoogwaardigheid den Aartsbisschop en met den oorlof der eerwaarde Pastors van de verschillige parochien is deze omzendbrief uitgevaardigd geworden voor uitdeeling onder het bestuur, van

SOUVENIR.

het ondergeteekende komiteit van beschikkingen, door den Hoogeerwaarden Aartsbisschop benoemd om deze belangryke ceremonie te geleiden.

Zeer eerw. Mgr.　John M. Farley, President.
　Zeer eerw. Edw. McKenna, Landsdeken.
　Zeer eerw. W. L. Penny, Landsdeken.
　Zeer eerw. Denis P. O'Flynn, Landsdeken.
Eerw. James W. Power.　Eerw. John F. Kearney.
Eerw. John A. Gleeson.　Eerw. Albert A. Lings.
Eerw. Nicolas J. Hughes.　Eerw. James J. Flood.
Eerw. Charles R. Corley.　Eerw. M. J. Lavelle.
　　　Eerw. N. N. McKinnon, S. J.
　　　Eeerw. Andrew Ziegler, C. SS. R.

Τοποθέτησις τοῦ Ἀκρογωνιαίου Λίθου τῆς
Νέας Ἱερατικῆς Σχολῆς τοῦ Ἁγίου Ἰωσήφ
ἐπὶ τοῦ Λόφου τοῦ Ὀυαλεντίνου, πλησίον τοῦ Ἰουβουδίου Στασίμου τοῦ Σιδηροδρόμου Νέας Ὑόρκης-καὶ-Βορρᾶ.
Κυριακῇ, τῇ δεκάτῃ ἑβδόμῃ Μαΐου, ὥρᾳ τρίτῃ, μ. μ.

Ἐν τῷ Ἀρχιεπισκοπείῳ, 452 Μαδισῶνος Λεωφ.
Ἐν Νέᾳ Ὑόρκῃ, τῇ 25 Ἀπριλίου 1891.

Τῷ Καθολικῷ Λαῷ τῆς Ἀρχιδιοικήσεως τῆς Νέας Ὑόρκης.

Ἡ Παντερότης αὐτοῦ ὁ Αἰδεσιμώτατος Ἀρχιεπίσκοπος προσκαλεῖ πάντας τοὺς Καθολικοὺς τῆς Διοικήσεως ἵνα παρῶσιν ἐπὶ τῇ καθαγιάσει τοῦ ἀκρογωνιαίου λίθου τῆς νέας Ἱερατικῆς Σχολῆς τοῦ Ἁγίου Ἰωσήφ, κατὰ Κυριακήν, τὴν δεκάτην ἑβδόμην Μαΐου, ὥρᾳ τρίτῃ μ. μ., ἐπὶ τοῦ λόφου τοῦ Ὀυαλεντίνου, πλησίον Ἰουβουδίου Στασίμου, ἐπὶ τοῦ Σιδηροδρόμου Νέας Ὑόρκης-καὶ-Βορρᾶ. Τελεσθήσεται αὕτη ἡ σεμνή ἀκολουθία ὑπὸ τῆς

Πανιερότητος αυτού, ο δε καλλιρρήμων και πολυμαθής Αρχιεπίσκοπος Ρώαν της φιλαδελφίας εκφωνήσει λόγον κατάλληλον. Πάσαι αι Καθολικαί Αδελφότητες ταύτης της Διοικήσεως επισήμως παρακαλούνται ίνα μετασχώσιν της τελετής. Από του καιρού της θεμελιώσεως του περικαλλούς Μητροπολιτικού Ναού ημών μέχρι τούδε, ουδέν εγένετο σύμβαν τόσον σημαντικόν διά τά συμφέροντα ταύτης της Διοικήσεως όσον η καθίδρυσις ταύτης της νέας Ιερατικής Σχολής. Επί πολλά έτη οι ιερείς εμαθητεύθησαν εν τη Επαρχιακή Σχολή εν Τρωία. Ένεκα δε της ατοπίας της θέσεως διά τε τον Επίσκοπον και διά τους ιερείς, απεφασίσθη συμφώνως πρός τά διδάγματα και τάς συμβουλάς της Ιεράς Τριδεντινής Συνόδου, ίνα καταστανθή εντός των ορίων της Διοικήσεως ημών Ιερατική Σχολή ήτις έσται υπό την άμεσον επίβλεψιν του Επισκόπου, άμα και ευπρόσιτος τοίς ιερεύσι. Επιτηδειοτάτην θέσιν εξελέξαμεν επί του λόφου του Ουαλεντίνου, εν τω προαστείω Υόνκερς, απέχοντι δεκαέξ στάδια από των βορείων ορίων της πόλεως Νέας Υόρκης, και προτιθέμεθα νά ανεγείρωμεν εκεί οικοδόμημα άξιον ημίσεως εκατομμυρίου δολλαρίων. Καλώς γιγνώσκουσιν οι πιστοί ημών την απαραίτητον ανάγκην ιερέων πεπαιδευμένων άμα και θεοσεβών, αφ' ου εκ της Ιερωσύνης πηγάσει η πνευματική ζωή του Λαού. Δι ο οι Καθολικοί πανταχού του κόσμου ευαριστούνται ιδόντες τους δοκίμους του ιερατικού αξιώματος καλώς 'ανατρεφομένους καί μορφωμένους, καί πάντοτε διακρίνονται 'ως γενναίως παρέχοντες 'όσα 'ενδέχεται κάλλιστα μέσα διά τήν παίδευσιν καί συντήρησιν τών 'ιερέων 'αυτών. Τούτων δέ τών γενναίων προτερημάτων μετέχει καί 'ο λαός ταύτης τής διοικήσεως. Όθεν καί 'επικαλούμεν 'αυτούς νά βοηθήσωσιν τους 'ιερείς 'αυτών 'ίνα πανηγυρισθή 'αύτη 'η τελετή 'αξίως 'εαυτών, 'αξίως τού μεγάλου 'εγκαινισθησομένου 'εκπαιδευτηρίου, 'αξίως καί τού πεφιλημένου 'Αρχιερέως 'ημών, τώ 'οποίω παραγενήσεται 'αύτη 'η 'υψίστη δόξα τής καταθεμελιώσεως Σχολής 'ήτις προηγουμένως διά ταύτην τήν 'ευρυτάτην Διοίκησιν πεπαιδευμένους καί 'αφωσιωμένους 'ιερείς 'οίτινες διαδέξονται τους νύν 'όντας 'όταν 'ούτοι τύχη χρησάμενοι 'ανθρωπίνη 'ενθένδε 'εις 'αμείνων παρελεύσονται. Διά τής παρουσίας 'αυτών 'εις ταύτην τήν τελετήν 'ο λαός 'ημών δημοσίως 'επιδείξει τήν τέρψιν 'ην 'αισθάνονται 'εν πράγματι τόσον στενώς συνδεδεμένω τή πνευματική 'ευδαιμονία 'αυτών.

Μετά τής 'επιδοκιμασίας τής Παντερότητος 'αυτού τού 'Αιδεσιμωτάτου 'Αρχιεπισκόπου, καί μετά τής συναινέσεως τών 'Αιδεσίμων 'Εφημερίων τών διαφόρων 'Ενοριών, 'αύτη 'η 'εγκύκλιος κατεσκευάσθη διά διάδοσιν 'υπό τήν διεύθυνσιν τών 'υπογεγραμμένων Μελών τής Διατακτικής 'Επιτροπής τής διορισθείσης 'υπό τού Παντιερωτάτου 'Αρχιεπισκόπου πρός 'επίβλεψιν ταύτης τής σπουδαίας τελετής.

Αιδεσιμώτατος Μονσ. Ιωάννης Μ. Φάρλευ. Πρόεδρος.
Αιδεσιμώτατος Έδουάρδος ΜαχΚέννα, Δ. Θ.
Αιδεσιμώτατος Διονύσιος Η. Ω'Φλίνν, Δ. Θ.
Αιδεσιμώτατος Γουλιέλμος Ι. Πέννο, Δ. Θ.

Αιδ. Ίάκωβος Γ. Πούερ. Αιδ. Ιωάννης Α. Γκήσων,
Αιδ. Αλβέρτος Α. Λίγγς. Αιδ. Νικόλαος Ι. Λιούτς,
Αιδ. Ίάκωβος Ι. Φλώδ. Αιδ. Κάρολος Ρ. Κορλυ,
Αιδ. Μ. Ι. Λαβέλλ, Αιδ. Ν. Ν. ΜαχΚέννων, Α. Ι.
Αιδ. Ίωάννης Φ. Κάρνη. Αιδ. Ανδρέας Ζήγλερ, Α.Α.Α.Σ.

Σημείωσις.—Διά πληροφορίας περί Σιδηροδρόμων, τιμής σιδηροδρομικών εισιτηρίων, διαστημάτων, κ. τ. λ., όρα δευτέραν σελίδα.

اعلان

ان نيافة الحبر المفضل رئيس أساقفة الطائفة المارونية لما تراءى له درجة محبة لد يه يبرك قد امر بإجراء
تعميم أيام رعيته بأنه عراء الأحد الواقع في السادس عشرين نصف أيار الحالي يجري الاحتفال
كليا نسبي لوضع اول حجر من أساس المدرسة المرونية الكهنوتية التي عزمنا على بنائها في
هذلا بن جان، مقربين من محطة السكة الحديدية استاء... اللنقرى عن طريق وبوابة
الكنقري مرتلقوا، وقد وضعت هذه الدراسة تحت حماية القديس مار يوسف ولقبناها:

"مدرسة مار يوسف الكهنوتية"

... (نص غير واضح) ...

اعداد

هي من العقد عين فوائد ادخنا دت المدرسة الجديدة في كل موجوولاون
حسبنا اخبر موئلا بالوقت ما انتقله اليا محدث توارج السنين
الردمين قبله تشبها با حمالهم وبناءً على انتقله المدرسة
الاكليريكية العامة المباركة في ذهلوي) احمدمدن ولدية
نيويوركت لدا في ددى موقع وفاد مناصا هناك الى
لقانتين هين) متم مدينة من محلة (دون درى) في بيه
رومنهاى) الرانف شمالي نيويورك والبعيدت عنها زها يا
سلين وبناءً على فتن الحج ادوه من اتى سن المدرسة
كذبت لمارى بذا من استعاء هذت اسماء اله كئلة
الكاثوليكية من ساخف وهماء وهما طلاب دمنال
هذا ارضنه العظم اطاحتنا نوى بعد ندنن السمعة
الكاثرائية العظم والاستقالت به والسائد وجه الحاصة
ما هذا البت اذ دع نخرج النظرى على مدارك
الحدث وترضع لبان الغدانة والحارى فضى خبذا لفيروست
كرة فمالة في كرم المسيح وفي وجه الملدوث تا خذمها قرى
قرى الاستازة لمدينة النفيلة ونترها وموتن البى سلناهام
عليها والمراض عما شاها وتنفدرها اسلكة السرقة على
اخلاق الاستقامة والقت دختنى لوم الجى ادول يوم ارجد
الواقع (١٧ ايار ذلم الساعة السادسة عماري المهاد
ركبينركى مخطيا خلال الحفلة سياده المعال العدا منه
الارسيبينستوي ريان استعف فيد ذلنا فن اطهر لمعة عن
نذائد بيوت العلم واهمة هذه المدرسة والكنىسة للزطة
عليها والمنه الوحيدة ان يسمع صدى صونا العاق وطلى
المنلات وروايب اليا كمل من يجنرد العقبد ركبم الحسنات؟

ترجمة محدى ابرهيم بعنك +

קוֹל קָרֵא!

אֶל־בְּנֵי־אֱמוּנַת־הַכְּנֵסְיָה הַקַּתּוֹלִיקִית בְּמָחוֹז
נוּ־יָארְק.

לָבוֹא אֶל חַג יְסוּדַת בֵּית־מִדְרַשׁ הַכֹּהֲנִים
הֶחָדָשׁ, בְּגִבְעַת וַואלֶענְטִין, סָמוּךְ לִמְקוֹם עֲמִידַת
מְסִלַּת הַבַּרְזֶל דּוּנְוּוּדִיע בְּשִׁבְעָה עָשָׂר לְיֶרַח
מַאי, בַּשָּׁעָה הַשְּׁלִישִׁית אַחַר הַצָּהֳרָיִם.

*(Valentine's Hill, near Dunwoodie
Station, Sunday, May 17th, 3 p. m.)*

זֶה שָׁנִים רַבּוֹת כִּבְנֵי הַמָּחוֹז הַזֶּה הָיוּ מְחַנְּכִים
בְּבֵית־הַמִּדְרָשׁ בְּטְרוֹיַא, וְיַעַן כִּי רָחוֹק הוּא הַדֶּרֶךְ
לֹא יָכֹל הָיָה לְרֹאשׁ הַכְּנֵסְיָה מִנּוּ־יָארְק
וּלְיוֹעֲצָיו לָבוֹא שָׁמָּה כְּפַעַם בְּפַעַם וְלָשִׂים עֵינֵיהֶם

עַל הַתַּלְמִידִים. עַל־כֵּן הֻעֲתָה בָּאָרֶץ לְמַלֹּאות דְּבַר
וַעֲצַת־הַכְּנֶסֶת־הַגְּדוֹלָה בְּטְרִיְדֶענט וּלְהָקִים
בֵּית־מִדְרָשׁ בְּתוֹךְ גְּבוּל הַמָּחוֹז אֲשֶׁר רֹאשׁ
הַכְּנֵסִיָּה יוּכַל לְהַשְׁגִּיחַ עָלָיו וְגַם הַכֹּהֲנִים הָאֲחֵרִים
יוּכְלוּ לְבַקְּרוֹ כְּחֵפֶץ לְבָבָם.

לָזֹאת בְּמָקוֹם נֶחְמָד וְנָאוֶה בְּעִיר יָאנְקֶערְס,
רָחוֹק שְׁתֵּי פַּרְסָאוֹת מֵהָעִיר נוּי־יָארְק, יִבָּנֶה בַּיִת
גָּדוֹל וְהָדָר אֲשֶׁר הוֹצָאוֹתָיו יַעֲלוּ לַחֲצִי מִילְיָאן
דָּאלַּארְס. וּבְיוֹם הַנִּזְכָּר לְמַעֲלָה רֹאשׁ הַכְּנֵסִיָּה
מִנוּי־יָארְק קָארְדִינַאן יָשִׂית אֶת־אֶבֶן הַפִּנָּה לְהַבִּנְיָן,
וְרֹאשׁ הַכְּנֵסִיָּה מִפָּהִילַארְעלְפָהִי כַיַּאן אֲשֶׁר נוֹדַע
בְּכָל הָאָרֶץ לִהְיוֹת בַּעַל לָשׁוֹן לְמוּדִים מָהִיר,
יַבִּיעַ אֶת־הַדְּרָשָׁה, וְכָל הַחֲבֵרוֹת הַקַּתְלִיקִיוֹת
יִשְׁתַּתְּפוּ בְּחַג הַזֶּה. מִיּוֹם הִוָּסְדָה בֵּית הַתְּפִלָּה
הַגָּדוֹל בְּנוּי־יָארְק לֹא הָיָה יוֹם גָּדוֹל כָּזֶה לְטוֹבַת
הַמָּחוֹז, כִּי כֹהֲנִים מְלוּמָּדִים וּמַשְׂכִּילִים הֵמָּה מַעְיָן
נוֹבֵעַ, אֲשֶׁר מִמֶּנּוּ תּוֹצָאוֹת חַיִּים וַאֲשֶׁר הָרוּחָנִי.
וְעַתָּה אַתֶּם בְּנֵי הַכְּנֵסִיָּה הַיְקָרִים! תְּנוּ כָבוֹד

לְהַכְּנָסְיָה, לְרֹאשָׁהּ, וּלְכֹהֲנֶיהָ, וְהִתְקַבְּצוּ וּבֹאוּ בְהָמוֹן רַב אֶל־הֶחָג הַזֶּה; כִּי בְּרָב־עָם הַדְרַת־קֹדֶשׁ. וּבָזֶה תִרְאוּ בַּמָּה יָקָר בְּעֵינֵיכֶם כְּבוֹד־אֱמוּנַתְכֶם וְטוֹבַתְכֶם הַנִּצְחִי.

בְּשֵׁם רֹאשׁ הַכְּנָסְיָה מִמָּחוֹז נוּי־יָארְק.

הַכֹּהֲנִים הַמְסֻדָּרִים

י׳ פאַרלע, ע׳ מכּענא, וּ׳ פעני, יעקב פּאַרער,
א׳ לינגס, י׳ פלאד, כּ׳ לאַווּעלע, ד׳ אפּלין,
י׳ קערני, י׳ גליזאָן, נ׳ הודש, כּ׳ באַרלי,
נ׳ מכינזאָן, א׳ ציעגלער.

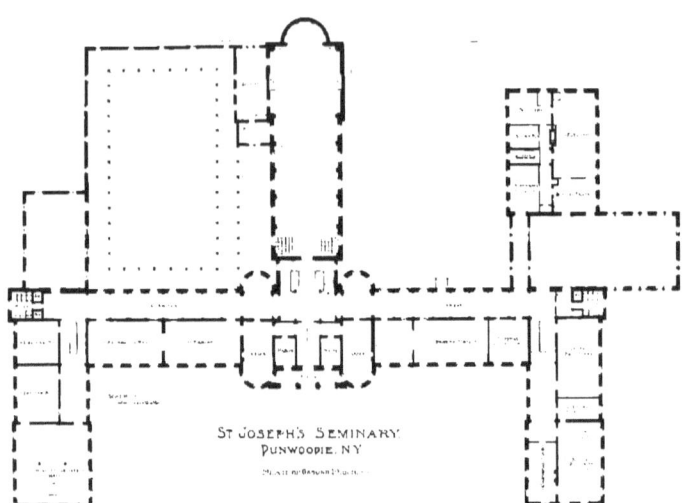

St. Joseph's Seminary
Dunwoodie, N.Y.

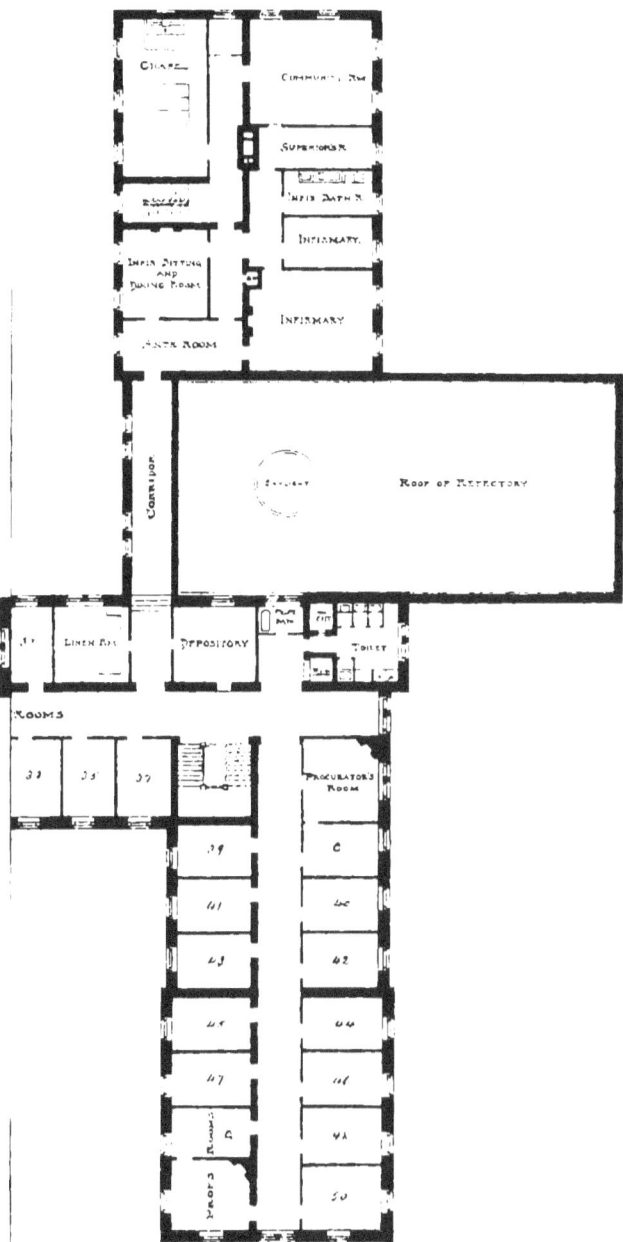

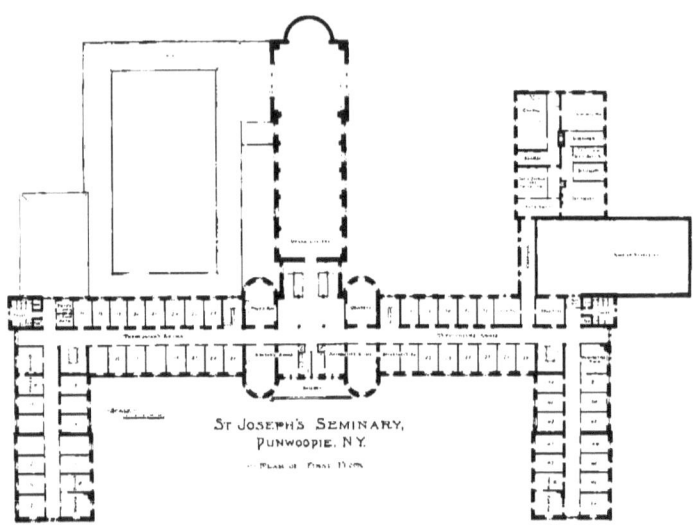

St Joseph's Seminary,
Dunwoodie, N.Y.
Plan of First Floor

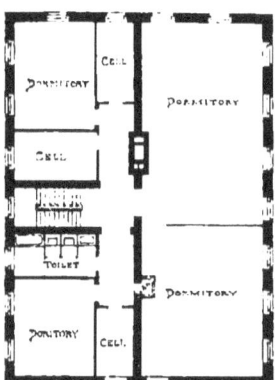

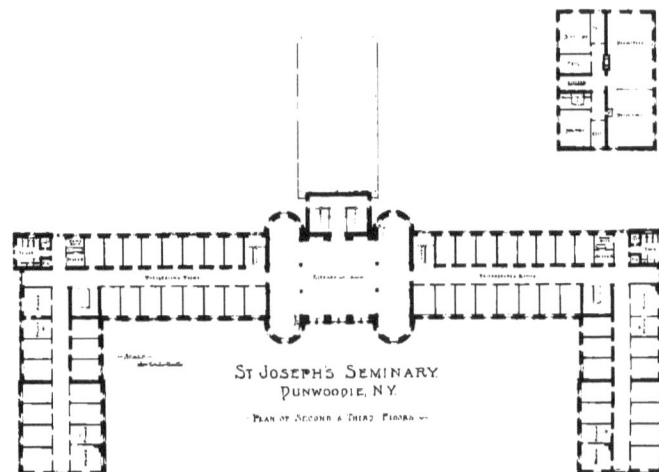

ST JOSEPH'S SEMINARY.
DUNWOODIE, N.Y.

Plan of Second & Third Floors

www.ingramcontent.com/pod-product-compliance
Lightning Source LLC
Chambersburg PA
CBHW032146160426
43197CB00008B/786